W9-CIN-759

RICHES IN CHRIST

Discovery Books

RICHES IN CHRIST

Ray C. Stedman

Word Books, Publisher
Waco, Texas

RICHES IN CHRIST

Copyright © 1976 by Ray C. Stedman. All
rights reserved. No part of this book may be
reproduced in any form, except for brief quotations
in reviews, without the written permission of
the publisher.

Quotations from the Revised Standard Version of the
Bible, copyrighted 1946, 1952, © 1971, 1973
by the Division of Christian Education of the National
Council of the Churches of Christ in the United States
of America, are reprinted by permission.

DISCOVERY BOOKS are published by Word Books,
Publisher in cooperation with Discovery Foundation,
Palo Alto, California.

ISBN 0–87680–850–X
Library of Congress catalog card number: 76–2860
Printed in the United States of America

First Printing, June, 1976
Second Printing, April, 1978

CONTENTS

INTRODUCTION

In the Epistle to the Ephesians, Paul sets forth for us the great fundamental facts of our faith in Jesus Christ, and gives us a detailed description of the riches that we have in Jesus Christ. The Apostle Paul emphasized these riches everywhere. As he traveled about the Roman Empire he came to colonies and cities whose people were spiritually and materially impoverished. Many of them were slaves. They had nothing of this world's goods. They were depressed, discouraged, beset with fears and anxieties, jealousies and hostilities. They were in the grip of superstition and filled with the dread of the future. They had no hope of life beyond death. It was the Apostle's great joy to unfold to them the riches available to them in Jesus Christ—riches which, if accepted as facts, would free them, would transform them and make them over into wholly different people, bringing to them a sense of joy and love and faith and radiant experience. That happened again and again, so that the Apostle had every reason to glory in these exceedingly great riches in Jesus Christ.

The Epistle to the Ephesians ought to be a treasure store to which we go repeatedly any time we get discouraged. I remember reading years ago about an old Navajo Indian who had become rich because oil had been found on his property. He took all the money and put it in a bank, and his banker became familiar with the habits of this old gentleman. Every once in a while the Indian would show up at the bank and say to the banker, "Grass all gone, sheep all sick, water holes dry." The banker wouldn't say a word—he knew what needed to be done. He'd bring the old man inside and seat him in the vault. Then he'd bring out several bags of silver dollars and say, "These are yours." The old man would spend about an hour in there looking at his money, stacking up the dollars and counting them. Then he'd come out and say, "Grass all green, sheep all well, water holes all full." He was simply reviewing his resources, that's all. That is where encouragement is found—when you look at the resources which are yours, the riches, the facts which undergird your faith. As we go through this letter to the Ephesians I hope you will read it in that way.

1

GOD AT WORK

Ephesians 1:1–14

Of all Paul's letters, the letter to the Romans and this one to Ephesians have affected me most profoundly. Both are attempts at a systematic and rather exhaustive setting forth of the whole Christian view of life and of the world. Others of Paul's letters deal with specific problems, and they are very helpful when we are involved with those problems. But these two deal with the whole sweep of truth, the great canvas of God's painting of reality.

As we begin this doctrinal portion of Ephesians, I hope your heart will be anticipating tremendous truth. I would like to urge you to read this letter through at least once with each chapter I have expounded. Read it through in various versions and in different ways. Let this truth come to you afresh in new and different language. I can guarantee that if you will do this faithfully until we finish our study, you will never be the same person again. This truth has the power to change you, and it will!

Ephesians has changed my life again and again. It was from this book that I learned how the body of Christ functions. The truth of the fourth chapter was strongly in my heart when I came to Palo Alto as a young man, fresh from seminary, and began to pastor a small group of people. It was my conviction that the ministry belongs to the saints, and that the business of a pastor is to help the people find their

9

ministries and to prepare them to function in them, and so discover the excitement of living as Christians where they are. This conviction was formative in the early years of Peninsula Bible Church and is still strongly emphasized.

It was from this letter that I learned as a young man how to handle the sex drive which God had given me, as he has given it to all of us, and how to live properly in a sex-saturated society. This letter is most practical in that way. It teaches us how to handle life as it is. Ephesians also taught me profound truths about marriage and family life, and I'm still learning in this area. It was this letter which taught me better than any other passage of Scripture how to understand the strange turbulence I often found in my own heart, the spiritual attacks to which I was subject. It taught me how to deal with my fears and anxieties and my depressions—where these were coming from and what to do about them. So this is a great and practical letter, and I urge you to become familiar with it and to make it your business to know the truth of Ephesians.

Let me share with you the experience of another person in this respect. This is from the introduction to a book by Dr. John Mackay, for many years the president of Princeton University.

I can never forget that the reading of this Pauline letter when I was a boy in my teens exercised a more decisive influence upon my thought and imagination than was ever wrought upon me before or since by the perusal of any piece of literature. The romance of the part played by Jesus Christ in making my personal salvation possible, and in mediating God's cosmic plan, so set my spirit aflame that I laid aside, in an ecstasy of delight, Dumas' *Count of Monte Cristo* which I happened to be reading at the time. That was my encounter with the Cosmic Christ. The Christ who was and is became the passion of my life. I have to admit without shame or reserve that as a result of that encounter I have been unable to think of my own life or the life of mankind or the life of the cosmos apart from Jesus Christ. He came to me and challenged me in the writings of St. Paul. I responded. The years that have followed have been but a footnote to that encounter.

So I would suggest that if you feel the need for change in your own life and for deepening your relationship with our Lord, you would do well to expose yourself in a very personal way to these teachings from Paul's letter to the Ephesians.

To All Christians Everywhere

This letter was written from Rome about A.D. 61, during Paul's first imprisonment there. It was written to the Christians in the Roman province of Asia. These were ordinary people—tradesmen, craftsmen, a few doctors and lawyers, some politicians—the general run of people. Many of them were slaves. The letter is commonly called the Epistle to the Ephesians but, as a footnote in the Revised Standard Version points out, many of the ancient manuscripts have a blank for the address of these saints.

Many scholars feel, therefore, that this is a circular letter which was written to many churches, probably those in the region of Ephesus. Some think it may have been addressed to the very churches to which Jesus had John address the letters in the book of Revelation, beginning with Ephesus and ending with Laodicea. It may be of interest to you to notice that in his letter to the Colossians Paul refers to a letter from Laodicea. Some feel that this is that letter. It was brought from Rome by the hand of Tychicus, to whom the Apostle dictated this great treatise. Circulated from church to church, and read in each one, it finally ended up in Ephesus where it was labeled "the letter of Paul to the Ephesians." At any rate, as we gather from Paul's footnote at the end, it is really a letter addressed to all Christians everywhere.

> Paul, an apostle of Christ Jesus by the will of God, To the saints who are also faithful in Christ Jesus: Grace to you and peace from God our Father and the Lord Jesus Christ (Eph. 1:1–2).

That salutation is the briefest in any of Paul's letters. There are just three simple things to which I will call your attention in passing. First, Paul's credentials: notice how he describes himself, "an apostle . . . by the will of God." An apostle was one sent with a message—a messenger. Paul gloried in the fact that he was an Apostle of Jesus Christ. And, as he tells us in his letter to the Galatians, the Lord Jesus appeared to him directly. Paul did not learn what he knew about the gospel by discussing it with the other apostles. Peter and James and John and others of the twelve were never teachers of the Apostle Paul. He learned the truth which he imparts to us here directly from Jesus Christ. And that is his authority.

Therefore when you read Paul's letters you are reading the words of an authorized spokesman for the Lord Jesus. He speaks by the authority of Christ, and he makes this clear in all his letters. I am sometimes amazed at the brazen temerity of people today who will read a section from one of his letters and say, "I don't agree with Paul." That makes me tremble. Paul is speaking as an apostle. An apostle is an authorized spokesman. What he says is what he has heard. So if you don't agree with Paul you don't agree with the Lord either.

Paul was always amazed by the fact that it was "by the will of God" that he was an apostle. He had no other glory in his life than that God, in the amazing wonder of his grace, had called a man who was such a bitter, intense, nationalistic persecutor of the church, had arrested him and changed him, and had sent him out to be an apostle to the Gentiles. Paul could never get over that. "Called by the will of God"—what a mighty influence this was in his life! He gives no other credentials. He doesn't refer to his training at the feet of Gamaliel, nor his Hebrew background and pedigree, nor the brilliance of his intellect, nor anything else. He simply says, "I'm an apostle by the will of God. That is the ground upon which I write."

No Plaster Saints

Then notice how these Christians are described: "saints who are faithful in Christ Jesus" (Eph. 1:1). *Saints* is a word that makes us all shudder a little. We don't like to be called saints because we have such an unrealistic concept of what a saint is. We think of them as being unreal—so beatific, so holier-than-thou, so unlike ordinary human beings. But the saints of the New Testament are not like that: They are people like us. Saints are people who are beset with struggles and difficulties at home and problems at work and troubles everywhere. They're normal people, in other words. But one thing is remarkable about them: they are different. That is really the basic meaning of this word *saint*. In the Greek it is a word derived from the word for "holy." And *holy* means distinct, different, whole, belonging to God and therefore living differently. That is the mark of the saint. It isn't that he doesn't have problems, only that he approaches them differently. He handles them in a different way, and has a different lifestyle.

Their characteristic is that they are faithful, which means, of course, that they can't quit. That's what a true Christian is—a person who can't quit being a Christian. When a young man called me recently to tell me how discouraged he was, how he'd lost his confidence in prayer because he felt no answer was coming, and how ready he was to quit, I said to him, "Well, why don't you just quit then? Give up. Stop being a Christian." I knew that if he tried to quit, the first thing he would discover was that he couldn't. And he knew it, too. The minute I said that, he acknowledged it: "You're right, I can't quit." As Paul will describe in this letter, we are sealed by the Holy Spirit of God, so we can't quit. That is a mark of a believer in Christ.

Then comes the invariable greeting of Paul to these groups of believers: "Grace to you and peace from God our Father and the Lord Jesus Christ" (Eph. 1:2). The two great heritages of the Christian are grace and peace. These are two things you can always have, regardless of your circumstances. *Grace* is all God's power, all his love, all his beauty, available to you. It is a marvelous term which wraps up all that God is and offers it to us. It comes from the same Greek word from which we get our English word *charm*, for grace is charming, lovely, pleasant.

Peace is freedom from anxiety, fear, and worry. These are

the two characteristics which ought to distinguish Christians all the time: grace—God at work in their lives; and peace—a sense of security, of trust. One man expressed it to me this way: "I've learned something new about trust: trust is not knowing, and yet being at peace, at rest." If you know what's going to happen, you don't have to trust. But trust is not knowing, and still being at peace.

From here the letter follows the usual structure of Paul's letters. The doctrine comes first—the teaching, the great revolutionary, radical facts that God is setting before us. Then comes the practice, the application, the working out of these facts in terms of the normal situations of life. Don't read these first three chapters as though they were mere theological gas. They are not. They are facts! They are what God says is real. They are what is actually happening in the world, and what is available to you. If you read them that way you won't be able to treat them as merely academic. You'll begin to found your life upon these facts and act upon them. That is why Paul always begins his letters by setting forth the radical facts of life as God teaches them.

It is also characteristic of Paul to gather everything up in one concise prefatory statement, as he does here, and then to break it down into its detail. The statement which Paul makes at the beginning of this letter summarizes all the great themes of Ephesians to which he will return again and again.

Blessed be the God and Father of our Lord Jesus Christ, who has blessed us in Christ with every spiritual blessing in the heavenly places [or, more literally, "in the heavenlies"] . . . (Eph. 1:3).

There are four elements in this summary that we must note. Paul begins first with the One who is behind all these blessings, the God and Father of our Lord Jesus Christ. That is his starting point. When a man begins with God you know that what he says will be in line with reality. Our problem is that we don't start our thinking with God; we tend to start it with ourselves and our own experiences, which is only a partial view of truth. Thereby we immediately narrow the range of our vision to what we are going through and what is happening to us, and we don't see it in relationship to the whole reality of life around us. Consequently we get twisted and deformed ideas of what is happening. The only proper way to view truth is to see it in relationship to all truth everywhere. There is only one way to do that, and that is to start with God. Only God is great enough to encompass all truth.

This is the difference between what the Bible calls "natural" thinking, as done by "natural man," and the spiritual thinking of "the spiritual man." Natural thinking is always limited, always wrong to some degree, because it isn't broad enough to handle all the facts. But spiritual thinking is God-centered, and therefore true, and to the extent that it is spiritual, it is true in every way. We need to learn to be spiritual thinkers about ourselves.

God Aims to Bless

The second element is the aim of the work of God. He sums it up in the twice-repeated word *blessed*. Blessed be God, and blessed are we with every spiritual blessing. God is aiming to bring about a world, a universe, filled with blessing. Everything occurs, as Paul says frequently throughout this letter, "to the praise of God's glory," i.e., in order that God should be praised, in order that his people should be so struck by the wonder of what has happened to them that their hearts reflect, without limit and without their being able to prevent it, the praise and the glory and the blessing of God.

This is nothing new, of course; we have all learned that God is to be praised and that we are to give thanks in all circumstances. But most of us think we must make ourselves praise God because his ego needs to be massaged every now and then by our praise. We think that unless we praise him, he won't operate. He will get mad at us and won't run things right, so we have to butter him up a bit to get him to work. Isn't that really the basis upon which most of us act, at least much of the time?

But that isn't what Paul is talking about at all. He is saying that God has done such remarkable deeds that once we fully understand them, there will be nothing we can do but stand in absolute awe and amazement and say, "You mean this is for me, Lord? I am overwhelmed! My God, how great thou art!" That is what God wants to produce—that sense of awe and amazement which causes us to stop and give thanks to a great and glorious God who has given us every spiritual blessing. In the verses that follow those blessings are listed for us, and we will look at them in more detail in subsequent chapters, but for now let me just gather them up for you briefly. First:

> . . . he chose us in him before the foundation of the world, that we should be holy and blameless before him (Eph. 1:4).

That is number one. It goes back before the beginning of time, before the foundation of the universe. Second:

> He destined us in love to be his sons through Jesus Christ, according to the purpose of his will, to the praise of his glorious grace which he freely bestowed on us in the Beloved (Eph. 1:5-6).

What a fantastic thing that is. We are members of the family of God, made to be partakers of the divine nature. Third:

> In him we have redemption through his blood, the forgiveness of our trespasses, according to the riches of his grace which he lavished upon us (Eph. 1:7-8).

Think of that! Our guilt is removed, utterly gone. Fourth:

> For he has made known to us in all wisdom and insight the mystery of his will, according to his purpose which he set forth in Christ as a plan for the fulness of time, to unite all things in him, things in heaven and things on earth (Eph. 1:9-10).

We have been taken into the secret counsels of the Almighty. He has unfolded to us what he plans to do, what he is going to accomplish in the future. We have been told something of the details of this plan. Then look at number five:

In him, according to the purpose of him who accomplishes all things according to the counsel of his will, we who first hoped in Christ have been destined and appointed to live for the praise of his glory (Eph. 1:11–12).

God has appointed us to be a demonstration of all these great truths, to live for the praise of his glory. Look at the sixth:

In him you also, who have heard the word of truth, the gospel of your salvation, and have believed in him . . . (Eph. 1:13).

All that, you see, comes as a part of the work of the word of truth. And then the last:

. . . [you] were sealed with the promised Holy Spirit, which is the guarantee of our inheritance until we acquire possession of it, to the praise of his glory (Eph. 1:13–14).

Those are the things that make life worthwhile. Without these great facts life is unbearable to man—desolate, dull, boring—we can hardly stand ourselves or each other. This is a list, if you like, of the incompetencies of man. Man cannot provide these. No political party can introduce them. They come from God, and God alone. No one else can give them to us, and it is absolutely impossible that we ever should achieve them by ourselves. They are the gifts of God, and they are all included in Paul's summary statement: We are "blessed in Christ with every spiritual blessing."

The third element of this great verse is that all this blessing is "in Christ." All this comes to us in Christ, in the Person and the work of the Lord Jesus himself. This fact is stressed again and again in this letter. No two words appear in it more frequently than "in Christ," or "in him." Over and over it is emphasized that everything comes to us through him.

We must learn not to listen to those who claim to have God's blessing in their lives, but who do not hold that Christ is central. They are deceived, and they are deceiving us if we accept what they say. The only spiritual blessing that can ever come to you from God must always come in Christ.

There is no other way that it can come. So if you are involved with some group which sets aside the Lord Jesus Christ and tries to go directly to God and thus claim some of the great spiritual promises of the New Testament, you are involved in a group which is leading you into fakery and fraud. It is completely spurious! For God accomplishes spiritual blessing only in Christ. Physical blessings are available "to the just and the unjust alike." But the inner spirit of man can be healed and cured only in Christ, and there is no other way.

Invisible but Real

Finally, notice where all this occurs: "in the heavenlies." Now that doesn't mean heaven, as we usually conceive of heaven. Paul is referring here to the present experience of these blessings. We are involved with the "heavenlies" right now. These *heavenlies*—and the term occurs throughout this letter and in other parts of Scripture—are really the realm of invisible reality, of things which are true about life in the world, in the cosmos, but which we can't see or touch right now. Yet, they are very real, and they play an important part in our lives now. This is what Paul refers to in 2 Corinthians 4: "We look not to the things that are seen but to the things that are unseen . . ." (v. 18). The heavenlies are unseen, invisible reality.

Do you remember the story in the Old Testament about Elisha and his servant? One day they found themselves surrounded by the armies of Syria. The servant looked out upon this vast enemy army and he saw the cavalry and the armed chariots. Fearfully he turned to Elisha and said, "Everything's hopeless! Look! We're surrounded! What shall we do?" Elisha said, "Fear not, for those who are with us are more than those who are with them." And he prayed, "Lord, open his eyes." And the Lord opened the young man's eyes so that he could see, ringing the horizon, all the fiery chariots of God, manned by hundreds of thousands of angels, and he realized the true situation. Those were the heavenlies.

Most of the important things of our lives are not visible. They can't be touched or seen or tasted or weighed or otherwise measured. They are not subject to the scrutiny of science, nor are they the subject of the philosophies of men, but they are there. We must recognize that fact. And it is in this realm that these great spiritual blessings are to be found. It is here that our life can be changed and we can become different people, by God's grace. All this will be developed in fuller detail as we go on into the letter.

For now, I just want to point out to you how Paul underlines the fact that it is God who does all this. This is not the activity of men that he is talking about. In this first chapter there is no demand for us to do anything. Later on, the question of human activity will come in, but not here. He is talking about what only God can do and what God alone has already done. All progress in the spiritual life comes by understanding the truth of what God has already done. Therefore, it is available to you the minute you understand it and grasp it.

Where the Action Is

It would be useful for you to take a pencil and underline the finite verbs of this passage. You will notice that they all refer to God. He chose . . . he destined us . . . he has made known to us his will. Go through the passage and what you will see highlighted is God at work. All around us in the world today men are doing things, and it is right and proper that they should. Men are to work and to plan, they are to dream and to hope, and they are to try to accomplish things. It is right for the government to try to govern and for statesmen to try to accomplish their goals. All of us have something to do. But what our age has tragically forgotten is that the only activity which will change anyone ultimately is God's activity, not man's. That is where we need to focus our thoughts, we need to see what it is that God is doing.

One of these days, as we all recognize but hate to admit, all the proud symbols of our civilization as we know it today will be brought low, to crumble into dust, to be lost in the debris of the ages. All the knowledge in which we pride ourselves today will be lost in some forgotten tomb. Man's glory will

fade. The accomplishments of our present day which give us
such satisfaction will become nothing but obscure references
in some future history, if anything at all. What will endure in
that day is the work of God. The great facts revealed in this
letter will still be as brilliant and untarnished in their reality
as they are today. Rudyard Kipling once wrote about the Brit-
ish Empire:

> Far flung, our navies melt away,
>   on dune and headland sinks the fire.
> Lo, all our pomp of yesterday
>   is one with Nineveh and Tyre.

America's greatness will also fade, as will Russia's, and that
of all the nations of the earth. But when that day comes, the
things which will be true are these great facts. Therefore if
we want to endure, if we want to lift our eyes above the plod-
ding circumstances of our own present experience to the
greatness of what God is doing, we must give our attention to
these great truths of God's design for us—planned before the
foundation of the world, begun even before there was an
earth, designed to reveal the greatness of God's grace, his
compassion, his tenderhearted love, his forgiving ability, his
power to restore. These truths are available through the one
Person who in all the scope of history is able to accomplish
what no other man could do, Jesus Christ himself—and resulting at last in the healing of all division and the breaking
down of every barrier.

In fact, Ephesians is all about how God is breaking down
the things that divide us. We are so aware of division today.
We are divided within our homes, divided in our work, divided into cliques and camps and nations, all against one another, with all the consequent hurt and injury and malice and
hate and prejudice. God is at work to remedy that. He is healing it. He has already begun. He is breaking down the barriers, removing the hate and enmity, restoring all things to
harmony.

Remember what Jesus said: "He who is not with me is
against me, and he who does not gather with me scatters"
(Luke 11:23). You can tell whose side you are on by the ef-

fect of your life. Are you gathering, or scattering? Are you healing, or hurting? Are you bringing together, or breaking up? Which is the direction of your life? Well, God's great movement in our lives as individuals, and in history at large, is to heal and make whole, and to bring together all things in Christ.

The exciting thing is, according to this letter to the Ephesians, that it has already begun in us. We are the first ones to set it forth. We, the Church, have felt the force of this great movement of God. We have found it in our homes—the barriers are beginning to break down there, the divisions are beginning to be healed. The harmony is beginning to emerge in our church life. And the more visible it becomes, the more the world will see God at work. This letter is all about how to allow this healing flow from the great God behind all things, through his Son Jesus Christ, to touch our individual lives and heal us of all our illness and injury. No wonder this great Apostle cries out, "Blessed be the God and Father of our Lord Jesus Christ, who has blessed us in Christ with every spiritual blessing in the [heavenlies]" (Eph. 1:3).

Are you a part of this scheme? Are you part of this family? Have you joined the family of God through Jesus Christ our Lord? If not, you can become a part of it right now. You can say, "Lord Jesus, here I am. I respond to your appeal. Enter my life and make me part of your family." And if you are already part of it you can give thanks to God.

Our Father, we pray that you will take away the dimness from our vision, the dullness from our understanding, and help us to comprehend these great themes which have changed the history of the world again and again, as men have grasped them. Save us from the folly of taking them for granted or of giving them no attention. But help us, Lord, young and old alike, to think deeply and seriously about these great statements, to understand that this is the way you are acting, this is the course of your movement through history. Lord, help us by your grace to rejoice, to lay hold of your provision, and to be responsive instruments in your hand; in Jesus' name we ask, Amen.

2

THE FOUNDATIONS

Ephesians 1:1–14

Look once again at this statement of God's grace that sums up all that Paul sets forth in the rest of his letter to the Ephesians:

> Blessed be the God and Father of our Lord Jesus Christ, who has blessed us in Christ with every spiritual blessing in the heavenly places . . . (Eph. 1:3).

If you want to keep the structure of the first chapter in mind, remember that we have this summary statement, followed by the more detailed description of the blessings, verses 4 through 14, and then beginning with verse 15, Paul's great prayer that his hearers would understand what he is telling them.

In the section before us now there is an unusual structure to which I'd like to call your attention. From verse 3 through verse 14 in the Greek text (not in the English) there is one complete, unbroken sentence. If you want to get the effect of it, take a deep breath and try to read it through in one breath. You will see how much Paul has crammed into this great sentence. It's almost as though he is taking a walk through a treasure chamber, like those of the Pharoahs of Egypt, and describing what he sees. He starts out with the most immediate and evident fact and tells us what that is.

Then something else comes into view and he puts that in. And glory flashes upon glory until he has piled up vast and almost indescribable riches in this tremendously complicated sentence.

Division of Labor

That is Paul's way of showing us how truth is interconnected. You can never touch upon some of these great themes without coming in contact with others, and soon you find yourself caught up with facts reaching out in every direction. That is how truth is. In the natural sciences, for instance, you can't study one subject without touching upon a great many others. This is the way God builds truth.

There is a rather simple way to divide this passage, however; that is, these blessings gather about the Persons of the Trinity. There is the work of the Father, the work of the Son, and the work of the Holy Spirit. In Ephesians 1:3–6 you have the work of the Father:

> Blessed be the God and Father of our Lord Jesus Christ, who has blessed us in Christ with every spiritual blessing in the heavenly places, even as he chose us in him before the foundation of the world, that we should be holy and blameless before him. He destined us in love to be his sons through Jesus Christ, according to the purpose of his will, to the praise of his glorious grace which he freely bestowed on us in the Beloved.

Then in verses 7 through 12 you have that which relates to the Son:

> In him [the Beloved] we have redemption through his blood, the forgiveness of our trespasses, according to the riches of his grace which he lavished upon us. For he has made known to us in all wisdom and insight the mystery of his will, according to his purpose which he set forth in Christ as a plan for the fulness of time, to unite all things in him, things in heaven and things on earth. In him, according to the purpose of him who accomplishes all things according to the counsel of his will, we who first hoped in Christ have been destined and appointed to live for the praise of his glory (Eph. 1:7–12)

How rich that language is concerning the Son, our relationship to him, and our present experience. Finally, in verses 13 and 14 you have the work of the Holy Spirit:

> In him you also, who have heard the word of truth, the gospel of your salvation, and have believed in him, were sealed with the promised Holy Spirit, which is the guarantee of our inheritance until we acquire possession of it, to the praise of his glory (Eph. 1:13–14).

Remember that these are all available to us in the realm which Paul calls "the heavenlies." As we have seen, that is not heaven, but rather the invisible realities of our life now. It reaches on into eternity, yes, but it is something to be experienced now, in the inner life. He is talking about your thought-life, your attitudes, where you feel conflict and pressure, struggle and disaster—that is part of the heavenlies. It is where we are exposed to the attack of the principalities and powers which are mentioned in chapter 6, those dark spirits in high places who get to us and make us anxious or hostile or angry. The heavenlies is the realm of conflict, but also the realm where God can release us and deliver us, where the Spirit of God reaches us at the seat of our intellect, our emotions, and our will. It is the realm of those deep urges which rise within us and create either a restlessness or a sense of peace, depending on their source. These blessings are yours in your inner experience now, if you are in Jesus Christ.

All of this, remember, comes to us in one great package: in Christ. If you are not a Christian you cannot possibly claim these benefits. They are not yours, they don't belong to you. You cannot buy them, you cannot discover them, you cannot sign up for a course about them in a university. You can't send away ten dollars in the mail and get a pamphlet that will lead you to them. There is no way you can appropriate them unless you are in Christ. But if you are in Christ there is nothing to keep you from having all of them, every moment of every day. That is why it is so important that we discover what they are.

These are fundamental truths which undergird us in every moment of our life. And unless you understand these facts you can't utilize them, you can't benefit from them. In that way they are like natural laws. The laws of nature operate regardless of how we feel—they are impersonal in that respect. I've been doing a bit of electrical work in an addition to my home, and I've discovered that electricity follows a pattern of its own and takes no notice of how I feel at the moment. That can be a shocking experience! Electricity is not in the slightest degree impressed with my position as a pastor of Peninsula Bible Church. It doesn't hesitate to retaliate for any violation of its laws that I commit. It is up to me to discover how it works, and then to respect it if I want to use it. The same is true of these great facts. They will do you not a particle of good if you don't discover what they are and believe them enough to operate on the basis of them.

Accept the Facts

To begin with, I would like to center on the two great facts mentioned here concerning the work of the Father. Here is the first statement: ". . . he chose us in him before the foundation of the world, that we should be holy and blameless before him" (Eph. 1:4). Here we are dealing with what theologians call the doctrine of election, i.e., the fact that God chose us to become Christians and to be in Christ before the very foundation of the world. If you begin to try to understand that truth your mind will boggle, because that is a fantastic statement. We struggle with it, we question it, and therefore I submit to you that we really don't believe it. If we did, it would show up in our actions, which is where the proof of our belief lies. We say, "How could this be? How could God choose us, and still offer us a choice?" And thus the struggle goes, between the doctrine of the free will of man and the sovereign election of God.

Many have wrestled with this great truth and have tried to explain it in various ways. Some say, "Well, God can foresee the future, and on the basis of what he knows we will do, he says, 'All right, I'll elect them to be part of my process.'"

That is not only too simplistic, but it is not what the Scriptures say. Others say, "Well, God sees what we will be when we become Christians. He sees the value that we will have toward him, and he chooses us on that basis." Again, nothing could be more unscriptural.

It is true that we are chosen of God. In John 6 Jesus said so himself, "No one can come to me unless the Father who sent me draws him" (v. 44). That's putting it plainly. You can't come to Christ unless you are drawn by the Father. God has to initiate the activity. Ah, yes, but in Matthew 11 Jesus made his appeal directly to the will of the individual, saying, "Come to me, all who labor and are heavy laden, and I will give you rest" (v. 28). That means it's up to us. We can never become Christians until we choose to come. So both of these facts are true. Though we can't reconcile them by our puny intellects, nevertheless we can accept them as facts. It is true that we must choose. The good news is offered to us, but unless we respond, we will never obtain the benefit of it. But if we do respond, if we come to Christ, if we believe in him, then we discover the great fact that it was God who began the process; it was he who chose us, and we have been drawn to him by his Spirit at work in our spirit. That is amazing. But it is the first thing that Paul wants us to know.

We also struggle with timing; he chose us "before the foundation of the world." Before we existed, before we ever took form seminally, let alone actually, we were chosen in him. Before there was an earth, no matter how far back in time you put it—billions of years into the past—you and I, as the very persons we are among the billions of people we could have been, were chosen in him. How could that be? Do you see how that boggles the mind?

We must realize that we are dealing with an eternal being, one with whom there is no past or future, but only an eternal present, only one great "now." He is able, therefore, to read our future as clearly as he does the past. He determines all things by the counsel of his will, as the next verse has it, bringing them to pass so that they all work together to accomplish what he wants done. We can only sit in amazed wonder and say, "Lord, how great thou art!"

"Chosen in him before the foundation of the world." Do you see what that does for our sense of identity as Christians? We are not afterthoughts in God's working. We are not accidental members of his body. There are no second class citizens in the church of Jesus Christ; we are all equal, chosen of the Father, selected to be members of his family, added to the new creation, the new order that God is producing in this world. What a fantastic privilege! We are chosen, not because of anything in us, as we'll see in a moment, but because of everything in him.

Restored to Good Working Order

The purpose of all this is that we are to be holy and blameless. God says he chose us for that reason, that we might be holy and blameless. Now I'd like to ask you a question. Are you holy? You aren't sure how to answer that, are you? These great facts are so revolutionary, so radical, that we hesitate to believe them. We hesitate to apply them to ourselves, despite the fact that they are true. The reason we hesitate is that we have such distorted ideas of what these words mean. We think that holiness is sanctimoniousness, resulting from a kind of theological de-worming process we must go through, and we don't want to claim that for ourselves. But it is not that at all. As a study in Leviticus reveals, holiness means wholeness, and wholeness means to be put to the proper use. When your body works the way it is supposed to, you are physically whole, and when your whole being functions the way it was intended to, you are holy.

Now, let me ask you this: Have you had your whole being restored to proper functioning? You may not always function properly, but do you have the capacity to do so? It is when we begin to understand these words that we can apply them and accept them.

Now let's look at the other one, *blameless*. Most people refuse to think of themselves as blameless because they know that they have done many things for which they ought properly to be blamed. That is, they have made choices, deliberately, against right, in spite of knowledge of the results. They have purposely done that which they know they ought not to have done. Therefore they feel they are to be blamed. But they are confusing this word with another; *blameless* does not mean "sinless." Never having done anything wrong is sinlessness. But you can be sinful and still be blameless. Do you know how? By handling your sin the right way!

Let's say you did something that injured someone else, and the full result of it was not visible to you when you did it. But afterward, when you saw how much you had hurt the person, you acknowledged it, apologized to him and did what you could to restore him. There would be nothing further you could do. From that point on you would be blameless. You would not be sinless—you still did it—but you also did all you could to handle it rightly.

The idea is the same with our offenses against God. What can you do about your sins, your evil? You can't go back and straighten it all out, no, but you can accept his forgiveness. You can acknowledge your need. You can put it back into his capable hands to straighten out the results of your sin. And when you've done that, you're blameless.

Now, are you blameless? Yes, of course you are, if you are in Christ. God has chosen us to learn this wonderful process of being whole and blameless.

These things are to be reckoned as true, even though you don't feel that they are. You say, "The sun rose this morning." It looks as though the sun travels around the earth. But you know better than that, don't you? You look out across the landscape and it looks flat, but you know better. Even though you can't see that the earth is round and revolves around the sun, you have learned to accept these facts despite your feelings. That is exactly what we are called on to do here. Accept the fact that God chose you in Christ to make you holy and blameless. And as you walk before him in his prescribed way, that is what you are. Rejoice in that great fact.

A *Change of Family*

Now look at the second great aspect recorded here of the work of the Father, which is related to the first:

> He destined us in love to be his sons through Jesus Christ, according to the purpose of his will, to the praise of his glorious grace which he freely bestowed on us in the Beloved (Eph. 1:5–6).

Here is a partial explanation of how God takes care of the past failures and shame of our lives in order to make us holy and blameless. He does it through a change of family relationship. He destined us to be sons—literally, he "foreordained us to sonship standing" or, as the Authorized Version puts it, to "adoption" as sons. We are familiar with the process of adoption. *Adoption* means leaving one family and joining another, leaving behind all that was involved in the first family and assuming the name, the characteristics, the resources, the history of another family. And this is the way Paul describes this relationship. We all belong initially to the family of Adam. We leave it, in Christ, and thereafter we belong to a new family, the family of Jesus Christ. We are no longer part of the family of Adam. Now that doesn't mean that we are not human; it means that we no longer need to be controlled by Adamic characteristics. We are still exposed to temptations to believe we are in Adam and to act accordingly, but we don't have to—that's the point. We've been transferred into a new family.

More than that, the emphasis is upon living as a full-grown, mature, responsible son. We are not put into this family as mere babes; we are put in as mature, grown-up individuals. As soon as we grasp the truth we can exercise it. In other words, to put it very simply, we are to live exactly as Jesus lived. He was a Son, the Son of the Father, and as such, a certain way of life was his. And now, in him, we have his lifestyle.

This is how Jesus described his own life: In John 6 he said, ". . . I live because of the Father" (v. 57). That is, "The

Father is my resource, my wisdom, my strength, my power. The Father is the secret of how I act and what I do and where I go. The Father is living in me and working in me. And in everything I do it is not I; it is the Father." He went on to say, "And I live because of the Father, so he who eats me [that is a beautiful figure for partaking of Christ, trusting in Christ] will live because of me" (v. 57). That is the secret of the Christian life. What a beautiful way to live! By the same method that Jesus lived, in the same way that he arrested the attention of humanity—this is the way that we are called upon to live. We have been made sons in him, like him, so as to share his life. It is this, you see, that pleases the Father. Isn't that amazing?

The rest of the statement deals with the why and how of this. Why should this be so? Most of us struggle with believing it because we say, "Why me? Why should he see anything in me which would motivate him to do that?" And of course that is our problem. It isn't that he sees anything in us. We make a serious error when we think that there is something in us which makes God choose us. No, the ground of his choice is the kind of God he is. "He destined us in love to be his sons . . . according to the purpose of his will, to the praise of his glorious grace . . ." (Eph. 1:5–6a). It is entirely God. His love began it, so he purposed it, literally, according to "the good pleasure" of his will. It gives him pleasure to do so, and it all results in joy, in praising him throughout all creation—"to the praise of the glory of his grace."

Joy Born of God

I saw a taste of that at Explo '72 in Dallas a few years ago. The thing above all else that impressed everyone who came to Explo was that all over the city there was an outburst of joy. It was infectious. There was a spirit of cheerful happiness no matter what happened. The young people, particularly, went all over the city and met everything and everyone with a smile or a "Praise the Lord!" Even the police of Dallas were impressed by this. One policeman said, "I've been treated like a human being for the first time in my career," and he couldn't get over the fact that it was young people who were treating him this way. Another, a guard at the Cotton Bowl, said, "I've been shoved 22,000 times this week, and everyone said 'Excuse me' when they did it."

Why? Because the joy was born of God. It was not coming from the circumstances—they were unpleasant, at times. Kids were living in tents, and sleeping on the ground, and often didn't have enough to eat. I met some who hadn't eaten for two or three meals, but their joy was undiminished. I watched the rain pour down upon thousands of them in the Cotton Bowl and not one of them complained; they just enjoyed it thoroughly. That is what God is after—to increase joy.

A woman who is in constant pain told me one time something of the struggle this pain has meant in her own life. She told me how she has cried out, "Why?" and has been assaulted with temptations to bitterness and resentment because she can't do what she'd like to do. She told how this had all reached a crisis about a year before, when she finally said, "Lord, I can't take this! It's too much for me! But, Lord, you seem to expect me to take it. No matter how much I pray, nothing seems to happen. But I just can't do it. So I give it back to you, Lord. If I'm even going to be able to exist, you've got to do it. You've got to uphold me, and somehow you've got to make me able to obey you and to reflect what you want me to be." And she said that there was born in her heart a sense of joy she couldn't explain. But that joy has remained. The radiance on her face as she told me about this was sufficient evidence that she was not trying to pull my leg. She was experiencing joy, unbroken joy—the praise of God's glorious grace—in the midst of pain and suffering, disappointment and frustration. That is what God is training us for. He has destined us to be the kind of sons his Son Jesus Christ is, according to the purpose of his will.

Finally, there is just one word on how all this grace has come to us, which introduces the next section which we will take up in the next chapter. It is "freely bestowed on us in the Beloved." The word is, God *engraced* us. He came to us in Christ, he poured it all out in Christ. Jesus was sent of the Father; that is the mark of his love. He came to be poor, he came to be misunderstood, to be opposed and hated, to be spat upon, to be cruelly beaten and finally crucified, so that we might be rich. Remember how Paul puts it in 2 Corinthians 8:9:

> For you know the grace of our Lord Jesus Christ, that though he was rich, yet for your sake he became poor, so that by his poverty you might become rich.

Now, my question is: Are you enjoying your inheritance? Do you wake in the morning and remind yourself at the beginning of the day, "I'm a child of the Father. I've been chosen by him to be a member of his family. He imparts to me all the richness of his life. His peace, his joy, his love are my legacy, my inheritance from which I can draw every moment of life, and have them no matter what my circumstances may be?" Do you trust in these unseen things which are real and true? Because if you do, when you trust in God's grace to be your present experience, you can know of yourself what the Father said three times about his Son Jesus. God the Father, looking down at you can say, "This one—this is my beloved child in whom I am well pleased." That is our inheritance.

Our heavenly Father, we thank you for these vast truths. We pray that our understanding may be made equal to them. We can't grasp them properly apart from the work of your Spirit, and we pray that you will open our eyes and help us to see that these things are true indeed, that they undergird our lives. And as we venture out upon them, as we dare to apply them to ourselves, you will take them and make them lead us into the liberty of the children of God, so that we will be free men and women—free, despite the circumstances under which we live, and despite the people with whom we have to work. We are a free people. We thank you in Jesus' name, Amen.

3

LIBERATED!

Ephesians 1:7–8

The Father's work on our behalf, according to Ephesians 1:3–6 was to choose us before the foundation of the world so that he could make us holy and blameless—whole and fully healed. He also reached out for us and drew us into his family, so that we now partake of his own nature. We have been made sons of God!

As we come to verse 7, we move to the work of the Son, the second Person of the Trinity, as he actually accomplishes what the Father has decided upon. The act of deciding was the Father's; the act of accomplishment is the Son's. The first stage of his action is given to us in verses 7 and 8:

> In him we have redemption through his blood, the forgiveness of our trespasses, according to the riches of his grace which he lavished upon us.

When I first worked through this passage I chose the title "Under Construction" because I was so impressed with the fact that all that is happening here is still going on. It is not something true only of our past; it is happening in our present. You can hear the sound of the sawing of boards and the pounding of nails, as God builds his church in the midst of the world today. It is true that we are under construction.

But I decided to change the title because of one Greek

word which appears in this passage, which focuses so marvel-ously on the first stage of this process. It is translated "re-demption," but that term has become "theologized" (which is another word for partially decayed!) so I'd like to use a modern equivalent: we have been *liberated*. The idea is that we've been set free. That is what the Apostle is trying to bring home to us.

Useless Until Purchased

This word brings to mind a picture of a slave market, which was a common sight in the Roman Empire, where human beings were offered as chattel for sale to anyone who could pay the price. Paul's idea here is that we were once bound as slaves in a great slave market. And Jesus came, paid the price, bought us, and restored us to usefulness. Until a slave is purchased, he is no good to anyone. But we who were useless have been purchased and freed in order to be useful and fruitful to Someone.

We still use the word redeem in that sense in connection with a pawn shop. When I was a student at Dallas Theologi-cal Seminary I used to spend my summers in Pasadena, Cali-fornia working in the Lincoln Avenue Presbyterian Church. We would drive out at the end of a school year and, as was always the case in those days, we had very little cash. All our accumulated savings went to buy the gasoline for the trip, and we always arrived absolutely flat broke. Usually we had spent the last of our money four or five hundred miles back and had gone without a couple of meals and slept in the car. There would be a week or sometimes two until my first check arrived, so I always had to pawn something. The only thing of value I had, besides my wife, was my typewriter. So the first thing I did in Pasadena was to take my typewriter down and pawn it. The pawnbroker and I became good friends as the summers went by. We would live on that money until my first check came, and then I'd redeem the typewriter.

Now, for that two-week period the typewriter was abso-lutely useless. I had no right to use it; the pawnbroker had no right to use it, and he couldn't sell it to anyone else. It was in hock. That is the picture Paul gives here. When I bought the typewriter back, redeemed it, it was restored to usefulness. Do you ever think of yourself that way? In our natural human condition we are useless for whatever God has designed us. There is no way we can achieve the sense of fulfillment we long to have.

I know a lot of people who resist this idea. They say, "Look at non-Christians. You talk as though only Christians achieve anything, but look at the non-Christian world. Look at how many skilled, talented, and able men there are, at how many things they can do. Why do you talk like this?" But there is a considerable difference between achievement and fulfillment. You can achieve a lot of things without Christ, but they don't satisfy. There is no sense of usefulness; it all seems to be wasted. There is within a kind of subtle, haunting reminder that this is all going to disappear some day, and that your contributions are only going to be blown up in the end. In any enduring sense, they are a waste of time.

I remember years ago, when I was teaching a home Bible class, the host and hostess invited their neighbor from across the street. He was an outstanding engineer, a brilliant man, who prided himself upon his own accomplishment. He had told them on several occasions that he had no need of God, no need of religion in his life. But he consented to come this evening because, as he told them, he'd be the devil's advocate. He came in a little late—the class had already started and I was already speaking—and he announced himself with a little obvious arrogance and said, "I'm so-and-so from across the street, and I've come in to be the devil's advocate." I said, "Well, you're welcome. Curl your tail around the chair and sit down. We'll be glad to have you." He spent most of the evening challenging the statements that were made, trying to disprove them. But it was obvious that he was at least curious, and perhaps hungry for truth in spite of his attitude.

I had a number of contacts with him afterward, and talked with him at great length. But he always insisted that he didn't need God at all. Then I learned that he had cancer, and we prayed that God would use this to show him that his achievements, in the light of that which is enduring, were worthless. His money and his brilliance could never buy what he really needed and wanted. Finally, I received word that he had committed suicide. His tragic end is eloquent testimony to what Paul is trying to say to us here. Achievement is not fulfillment, but when Christ comes in, there is fulfillment. In our natural humanity, we are forlorn, abandoned, without practical value, for though we obviously have great potential, we are unable to find fulfillment. Into this slave pit, says Paul, Jesus came, and he struck off our fetters and set us free. He liberated us and restored us to useful, fruitful, eternally significant living.

On one of our trips to Texas not long ago, we had with us a delightful young man who was the only one in the group with a long, flowing beard and hair to his shoulders. He was a choice young man. He gave his testimony one evening and recounted how just two years before, following the pattern of so many youths up and down the West Coast, he had gotten into drugs. He was blowing his mind with heroin and LSD and other things, had tried to find satisfaction in sexual escapades of all types, and had sought some sense of significance living in a commune. There, in the midst of his dreary, lonely, desperate life, somebody told him about Jesus. He told us that in just a flash it dawned upon him what Jesus had done. It was as though scales fell from his eyes, and immediately he was delivered, liberated. He never went back to drugs from that moment. He cleared up his sex life, and straightened out other areas. And the joy and the radiance with which he told this story gave ample evidence that the glory of this liberation was still with him, and he was enjoying the fullness of it.

Now that we have been liberated, redeemed, what has happened, specifically? Paul amplifies it for us in this verse:

> In him we have redemption through his blood, the forgiveness of our trespasses . . . (Eph. 1:7).

What happened is that our trespasses, our sins, were forgiven. The Greek word for trespasses in this verse is a word which means our missteps, our stumblings, our tragic, hurtful blunderings in which we think we are doing something that will fulfill us, but we wind up bitter and disillusioned. But those stumblings have been forgiven. The Greek word for *forgiveness* means "dismissed." They have been set aside. They are no longer considered or taken into account; they are ignored.

Why We Hide

Here Paul is putting his finger on the chains that bind us in our enslaved condition. It is our guilty awareness of these deliberate acts and choices that operates to make us hide from God, and also from each other—and even from ourselves. It is our remembrance of these wrong deeds that makes us withdraw because we don't feel we'll be accepted. We think we're not acceptable to God because of our evil deeds, and we begin to feel uncomfortable about ourselves. We can't feel comfortable in the presence of others unless we know that they have done the very same things we've done. And so life begins to turn reclusive. We try to become self-sufficient. We don't want to be dependent upon anyone else. We become secretive, suspicious, independent, private, and thus also lonely and hurt, resentful, bitter and despairing. That is the pattern on which life is lived all around us, and which we know so well in our own experience.

But when Jesus comes into our lives he dismisses these trespasses. They are forgiven, set aside, and we hear him say to us, as he said to that unfortunate woman taken in the very act of adultery, "Neither do I condemn you; go, and do not sin again" (John 8:11).

Now how could he say it? On what ground could Jesus ever utter a sentence like that? How could he remain just and consistent with himself and yet set aside our guilt so completely? The answer, Paul says, is "through his blood." That is how it happens. All through the Scriptures you find that there is no forgiveness from God apart from that shameful episode of the cross.

The Point of His Death

The cross is not a pleasant thing. Blood is never pleasant. It is sticky, messy, sickening. There are people who cannot stand the sight of blood. This whole business of a bloody Savior is offensive to most people, because they do not understand why God insists upon blood before there is forgiveness. And yet there is no other way. Scripture is unanimous in its testimony. Without the shedding of blood there is no forgiveness of sins. Why? Because it is the blood that underscores the reality of our guilt. Jesus died because we deserved to die. And we really do deserve to die; that's the whole point! We are not merely well-intentioned people accidentally stumbling along into trouble. We know that somewhere, somehow, we are involved in these deeds—and deliberately so—and thus we deserve the judgment of God. Our consciences tell us this; we can't escape them.

Jesus died because he took our place. That is what the Scripture announces. He was not merely a substitute. It is always difficult for us to understand how an innocent person can die for a guilty one and set him free. But the Scriptures do not really teach that he was only a substitute. There is an identity involved. What Scripture says is that he actually *became* us. "For our sake he made him to be sin who knew no sin . . ." (2 Cor 5:21). And when he became what we are, God put him to death, because that is what we deserve. Scripture honestly faces right up to the fact of our guilt.

There is an idea abroad today that the gospel is considered good news because it tells us that men are not really to blame for their misdeeds. There is a school of behaviorism today which says that we can't help ourselves for what we did; we are the victims of our circumstances, or of our genetic makeup. Our genes are responsible, our pressures, our parents. It's not our fault. We had to do what we did; there was no way we could avoid it. But I want to say that if that is the case, then we are of all people most miserable. There is no escape from our guilt, because there is something deep within the human conscience which will not buy that proposition, will not settle for it. Our conscience continues to haunt us even though we try to repress it, and so we can never find the peace we're looking for. We know we're guilty. We know that we've consented willingly to these pressures, that we didn't just give in because it was the most convenient thing to do, we wanted to do it. We would have resisted attempts to stop us. There is no escape from a guilty conscience apart from the blood of Jesus, because it alone faces guilt squarely and does something about it.

Some time ago I ran across a quotation from Dorothy L. Sayers, who has done some very keen thinking in the area of theology. She says in her *Creed or Chaos:*

One of the really surprising things about the present bewilderment of humanity is that the Christian Church now finds herself called upon to proclaim the old and hated doctrine of sin as a gospel of cheer and encouragement. The final tendency of the modern philosophies—hailed in their day as a release from the burden of sinfulness—has been to bind man hard and fast in the chains of an iron determinism. The influence of heredity and environment, of glandular make-up and the control exercised by the unconscious, of economic necessity and the mechanics of biological development, have all been invoked to assure man that he is not responsible for his misfortunes and therefore not to be held guilty. Evil has been represented as something imposed on him from without, not made by him from within. The dreadful conclusion follows inevitably, that as he is not responsible for evil, he cannot alter it; even though evolution and progress may offer some alleviation in the future, there is no hope for you and me, here and now. I well remember how an aunt of mine, brought up in an old-fashioned liberalism, protested angrily against having continually to call herself "a miserable sinner" when reciting the Litany. Today, if we could really be persuaded that we *are* miserable sinners— that the trouble is not outside us but inside us, and that therefore, by the grace of God, we can do something to put it right, we should receive that message as the most hopeful and heartening thing that can be imagined.

That is exactly what Paul is saying. The gospel emphatically does not say to us that we are not guilty, not to blame.

What it says is that we are to blame. It faces us squarely with
our guilt, our complicity, our willing cooperation with the
forces that tempted us. It does not dodge it, it faces God's
just sentence of deserved wrath and says it is right, it is true.
But then, it argues, the price is fully paid. Fully paid! God's
integrity has not been violated. He is free now to love us to
the utmost degree. His justice has been upheld in the blood
of his Son.

No one can ever argue that God takes a light view of sin
when he sees the cross of Jesus. In all that bloody, gory episode there is marvelous testimony to the whole world that
God will never, ever put up with evil. But the cross argues
for us that there the price has been paid on our behalf. He
who took our place paid the full price, and therefore we are
free. God fully accepts me. There is nothing ever to hinder
him in the least degree. I can look my guilt in the face and
acknowledge it, admit the whole stinking mess, and point to
the cross and say, "That has fully taken care of it, and therefore there is no use talking about it any more. The cross has
settled it. I'm no longer what I once was because of that."

Paul calls that full acceptance "the riches of his grace."
God did it all; I did nothing to deserve it or merit it in any
way. But you notice that he uses an additional phrase which is
most significant. He says:

> . . . according to the riches of his grace which he lavished
> upon us (Eph. 1:7–8).

What does lavished mean? Well, when you lavish something upon someone you heap it on more and more. Lavished
means repeated portions, given again and again. That is very
important for us to realize. Paul is not referring here to the
time he was forgiven when he first became a Christian. In
fact, redemption of believers in the New Testament is always a present occurrence, and it is exceedingly important to
see this. I find that many Christians think their sins were
forgiven only when they were converted, when, for the first
time, they laid hold of the grace and the forgiveness that is in

Jesus Christ. Then God wiped out the past and gave us a clean slate, and from now on it is up to us to keep it clean. He gave us a new start once. Now we are to struggle to keep things straight. I tell you that if that is the case I'm hopelessly lost, and so are you, because I haven't been able to keep it clean since then.

No, there is an existential note here. Redemption is constantly being repeated, eternally present, occurring again and again. Whenever guilt strikes me, whenever I discover that I have lied to myself, as I do, deceived myself, told myself at one level that I was doing the right thing while at another level I was giving way to what I knew to be wrong, and loving it—whenever that happens, I must acknowledge it. That is essential! Immediately the accomplishment of Christ is available, has already availed for me, and I can rest once again in the full acceptance of God my Father.

Face the Facts

It is not that God has ever ceased accepting me at any time. His forgiveness was always present. But my ability to receive it hangs upon my willingness to face the facts and acknowledge them. The moment I do, I experience anew, afresh, again, the sense of liberation. I tell you, I need forgiveness daily, and daily I have it. I experience daily the joy of being set free, restored to usefulness.

Do you know what that means? It means, first, that God accepts me. He accepts me inspite of the way I've been living and the way I am right now. There is no quibble about it, no second-class citizenship involved; he fully accepts me. I am his son, his beloved son in whom he is well pleased; that's my identity from now on. And because of that, I find I can accept myself.

There is the key to self-acceptance. The reason we feel haunted with guilt is that we have never accepted and forgiven ourselves. But if we haven't forgiven ourselves it is a sure sign that we have never really accepted God's forgiveness. The moment I understand that God, who sees everything exactly the way it is, in utter, stark naked reality, says of me, "I am satisfied with you in the blood of Christ; you are accepted by me," then I have no right to say anything less about myself, and I can accept myself. That means that I can also accept you. I can accept the fact that you, like me, are not perfect, and that you need forgiveness too. And it becomes my privilege and joy to extend that forgiveness to you, to say: "That's okay, I'm not going to hold it against you. I'm glad to forgive you because I've been forgiven."

There are some who say this exploits this gospel of grace. They say, "If that's the case then I'll go out and do anything I please, sin all I want, and God is going to forgive it." But Paul argues in many of his letters that if you can say *that* about the grace of God, then you've never experienced it. If you can really say that you are going to go out and exploit his grace, then you've never known what it means to be forgiven. For if you truly believe, your reaction inevitably is, "What a tremendous thing that I'm free from inner tension and self-hatred!"

There is no anguish, no agony, like guilt. There is nothing that haunts us so, nothing that makes us so peevish and miserable and restless and upset with others as this terrible sense that we are inadequate people, that we are not worth anything. To feel that way means that we have not accepted ourselves on God's terms. But if you once sense that you are forgiven, healed, whole in God's sight, that all of your sin has been set aside, and that now you can accept yourself and regard yourself as a wholesome, adequate person, worth a great deal, made in the image of God, then you want to sing and rejoice and dance and shout to the heavens that at last you've been set free; and you have no desire to go back and add to that load of guilt again.

What a Wonder!

I once heard a Methodist minister close his message by telling us of an incident which had occurred the Sunday before. At the close of the service he asked a Young Life worker to come up and dismiss the service in prayer. He knew that this young man had discovered just the week before that he had terminal cancer. When he came forward he brought his guitar with him. He stood on the steps of the platform and said, "I'd like to give the benediction, but I want to sing it."

Before he sang he gave a brief word of testimony regarding his own life. He told of how he had been raised in the streets, had been kicked around, hadn't known any family life, had fallen early into drugs, had shot heroin for six years, and had destroyed most of the soundness of his body and laid the foundation for the cancer that came later. He told of how he had sold his body to men to be used homosexually, had made his living that way, and of how miserable and wretched he was in that situation, trying desperately to find some sense of meaning and worth. Then someone told him about Jesus, and he told of how Jesus had freed him. He had become a Young Life worker in order to share the Word with high school kids. Then he said, "I want to sing this song now as the benediction." He struck a few chords on his guitar and very simply he began to sing that old Sunday school song written by Philip Bliss:

> I am so glad that our Father in heav'n
> Tells of His love in the Book He has giv'n;
> Wonderful things in the Bible I see;
> This is the dearest, that Jesus loves me.
>
> Tho' I forget Him and wander away,
> Kindly He follows wherever I stray;
> Back to His dear loving arms would I flee
> When I remember that Jesus loves me.
>
> Oh, if there's only one song I can sing,
> When in His beauty I see the great King,
> This shall my song in eternity be,
> "Oh, what a wonder that Jesus loves me."

Oh, what a wonder that Jesus loves me! That is what gives us our sense of worth—our sins are forgiven, not only in the past but momentarily, day by day. Never, ever will our sins separate us from the love of God which is in Jesus Christ our Lord!

Our Father, we pray that these words may come home to our hearts with reality, and that we will understand that only in those areas of our lives where we have been forgiven do we have any standing in your sight. If there are areas of our life where we think we've made it, where we're already satisfying to you, where we've never needed to be forgiven, where we've been adequate, Lord, those are the very areas in which we stand condemned and ought to be ashamed. Forgive us our self-righteous spirits which often try to stand upon a phony righteousness, as though we were good in ourselves. Help us to take our place with the saints of all the ages and say these words, "We've been redeemed by Jesus' precious blood, and only that has paid an adequate price." We ask in his name, Amen.

4

THE MYSTERY OF UNITY

Ephesians 1:9–12

The great question with which men continually wrestle in our day, as they have all through history, is whether or not there is a purpose in the universe. Do the events of history make any sense? Is the record of human events, with its concatenation of tragedy and happiness and misery and heartache and joy, moving toward any one goal? Or is life, as Shakespeare had Macbeth describe it, "a tale Told by an idiot, full of sound and fury, Signifying nothing" (*Macbeth*, Act V, sc. 5)?

There are many people today who agree with Macbeth. Many respected voices say that there is no purpose for the universe. Many historians, scientists, and others, looking at life around us, at the human story, say that no plan is evident, no purpose discernible, through all the strange mixture of history.

In William Barclay's Daily Study Bible Series, he cites several English voices in this respect. Oscar Wilde, in one of his epigrams, said, "You give the criminal calendar of Europe to your children under the name of history." That is all he could see in history, a criminal calendar. G. N. Clark, in his inaugural lecture as president of Cambridge University, said, "There is no secret and no plan in history to be discovered. I do not believe that any future consummation could make any sense of all the irrationalities of preceding ages. If it could not explain them, still less could it justify them." And in the introduction to his *A History of Europe*, H. A. L. Fisher writes, "One intellectual excitement has been denied me. Men wiser and more learned than I have discovered in history a plot, a rhythm, a predetermined pattern. But these harmonies are concealed from me. I can see only one emergency following another, as wave follows upon wave, only one great fact with respect to which, since it is unique, there can be no generalization, only one safe rule for the historian —that he should recognize in the development of human destiny the play of the contingent and the unforeseen." And André Maurois said, "The universe is indifferent. Who created it? Why are we here upon this puny mud heap, spinning in infinite space? I have not the slightest idea, and I am quite convinced that no one else has the least idea."

Well, that is a common view in our day, but the Apostle Paul disagrees emphatically! His great statement in Ephesians 1:3–14 gathers up a tremendous array of facts which disprove that view. This statement cuts right across the thinking of the men in Paul's day and of the leaders of thought in our day.

In verses 9 through 12, in one vast and glorious sweep, the Apostle deals with the purpose of the universe:

> For he has made known to us in all wisdom and insight the mystery of his will, according to his purpose which he set forth in Christ as a plan for the fulness of time, to unite all things in him, things in heaven and things on earth. In him, according to the purpose of him who accomplishes all things according to the counsel of his will, we who first hoped in Christ have been destined and appointed to live for the praise of his glory.

That is another of the vast and complicated statements in which the Apostle crams together truth relating to one great, central theme—the purpose of God in what is happening today. It is here that we begin to understand the world around us and the course of history as it rolls on. In order to understand it we must take this statement apart. I find four major divisions in it.

The Hidden Purpose

There is first the secret itself, "the mystery of his will," the hidden purpose of God. You notice that Paul describes it as a mystery. A mystery, as you may recall, is a secret which only God understands, and which men desperately need to know. Mysteries are the answers to the great questions which continually throb in the human heart. But no ordinary human enterprise—no course of instruction, no university curriculum, no scientific investigation—will ever reveal these secrets. Only God is able to tell us the answers. This is the sort of mystery spoken of here.

In 1 Corinthians 4 Paul reminds us that we Christians have been made stewards, or dispensers, of the mysteries of God. It is up to us to grasp them, understand them, and speak out about them. What is wrong in the world of our day is that the church has not been speaking about the mysteries which belong to it, and therefore the world is in confusion and darkness. It is up to us to tell these forth.

The second division, a very important one, is the way by which the mystery of God's will was made manifest. The third is the time in which it is to be fully manifested. And the fourth is the part which we will play in accomplishing it, our part in this tremendous procedure.

First let's look at the great secret which Paul sets before us, found in the latter part of verse 10: "to unite all things in him [Christ], things in heaven and things on earth." That is what God is doing in history. He is working to unite all things in Christ. That is rather an amazing statement, because it looks as if exactly the opposite is occurring in history; things seem to be falling apart. Paul has an answer for that, but first he wants us to understand the direction in which God is moving; he is going to unite all things in him.

When Paul says "all things," he means all things. In fact, he amplifies it: "Things in heaven and things on earth." Things in heaven, the invisible realm of reality, are the forces at work in our lives which we can't see or taste or touch or feel, both evil and good. In this realm, the evil principalities and powers are struggling with the angels and the forces of good. "Things on earth" include all the visible forces of this world, the struggles between nations, and strife among individuals. All these struggles will cease and all will be united together. The Greek word for *unite* means "to head up"; all things will relate to Christ as a body relates to its head. Then he will be the director, the supreme operator, of all things, both in heaven and on earth.

Paul describes the process by which Christ becomes the head in his letter to the Philippians. The first step was "disglorification." Our Lord emptied himself of the glory that was his though he was equal with God, took upon himself the form of a servant, and was born in the likeness of man. Then he humbled himself and became obedient unto death, even death on a cross. "Therefore," Paul writes, "God has highly exalted him and bestowed on him the name which is above every name, that at the name of Jesus every knee should bow, in heaven and on earth and under the earth, and every tongue confess that Jesus Christ is Lord, to the glory of God the Father" (Phil. 2:9–11). God is moving in that direction, and he is working toward this end in the time and space continuum in which we live.

A Divided World

It certainly doesn't look that way though. It is evident on every side that we are living in a divided world. We are out of step with nature; something has come between us and the animals—they hate us, fear us, run from us. We destroy them, eliminate them gradually but steadily from the face of the earth. We pollute the rivers and darken the skies and build garbage heaps around us that we don't know what to do with. We know we are doing this, but we don't know how to stop it, because this is a divided world. Something is at work to keep us from being in harmony with the world of nature in which we live.

We are also at war among ourselves, with nation against nation, class against class. Struggle and strife and division are taking place on every side. Our newspapers are full of it.

Each one of us is a walking civil war. We fight within ourselves. We want to do something good, but at the same time we want to do exactly the opposite. We want to have our cake and eat it too, and we struggle constantly in this way.

The great thought which Paul drops on us in this passage is that Jesus has come to stop all that. He has come to heal the broken relationships, to end the strife, to still the bitter, angry, hateful words that men say to one another. He has already started. He has begun healing, binding up, bringing all the divisions to a close. He himself said, "He who is not with me is against me, and he who does not gather with me scatters" (Luke 11:23). He has come as a healing force into the world to mend all the damage and bind up all the broken hearts. Paul makes a point of that. He says this great fact was made known to us by the life of Jesus.

> For he has made known to us in all wisdom and insight the mystery of his will, according to his purpose which he set forth in Christ . . . (Eph. 1:9).

It is very important to see that; you will never understand the purpose unless you understand the way it was made known. It was "set forth in Christ." There is something very remarkable hidden in this statement. This is the way we can come to understand what is happening in the world of our day, the events of today. If you understand what this "setting forth" is, and how it works, you can make sense of the events which otherwise don't make sense at all.

You must never read your newspaper as unrelated to what God is doing. He is working in this world. Every event is brought about, and finds its meaning by the way it fits into his plan. So what part does each headline play? How do you understand it? Where does it fit? That is exactly what Paul is dealing with here—how to read your newspaper intelligently, how to see where these current events fit into the program and the working of God in the affairs of men.

This mystery has been made known to us, he says, "in all wisdom and insight." These two words, *sophia* (wisdom) and *phronesis* (insight), were well understood by the Greek world. *Sophia* was the passion of the philosophers. They loved to try to find the secrets of life and to seek after wisdom. *Phronesis* was the common-sense, practical application of these to the problems of life. So Paul says that this mystery of God's will came to us through wisdom and insight made known, or set forth, in Jesus Christ. There is your clue; it is in Christ that you see how this works.

If you think through the ministry of Jesus you can see what he is getting at. The end results of the ministry of healing which Jesus came to do are visible in his *works*. This is why he did his miracles. There is that beautiful passage in Isaiah 35 where Isaiah predicts that God will come to us. And what does he say will be the results?

> Then the eyes of the blind shall be opened,
>   and the ears of the deaf unstopped;
> then shall the lame man leap like a hart,
>   and the tongue of the dumb sing for joy (Isa. 35:5–6b).

There will be healing manifested in nature on every side.

That is what happened when Jesus came. He began to heal. He opened blind eyes and touched lame men and made them well. He mastered the forces of nature—he stilled the storm, walked on water, changed water into wine. He delivered the oppressed from the realm of Satan. He set men free, he liberated them, and healed the hurt of their lives. This was but the visible demonstration that the end result of his work, which he began then, would finally and ultimately be seen everywhere.

Revolutionary Principles

Now follow closely: the principles by which this healing would take place in men's spirits, as well as their bodies, are set forth in the *words* of Jesus. That is why it is so important to listen to his words. The gospel records of the messages and sermons of Jesus are vitally important! In these, he has declared to us the radical approaches to life, the revolutionary principles, which will produce a new creation, and are producing it right in the midst of the destruction of the old.

Have you ever really seriously listened to the words of Jesus? Take the Beatitudes, for instance. "Blessed [happy], are the poor in spirit . . ." (Matt. 5:3). Do you ever feel that way? When you are poor, impoverished in spirit, when you feel as if you have nothing left, drained dry, with no riches of spirit remaining to you at all, are you happy? Do you go around rejoicing and singing, "Oh, how great it is that I'm so poor in spirit!"? No. We say we're depressed, and we often react with bitterness. But listen! Jesus says that is a golden moment. "Blessed [happy] are the poor in spirit, for theirs is the kingdom of heaven" (Matt. 5:3). At that point, at that place, you are in a position to receive riches from a different source and by a different process than is available at any other place, any other point of your life. There you are able to take them, and nowhere else.

"Blessed [happy] are those who mourn, for they shall be comforted" (Matt. 5:4). Do you ever think of yourself that way? Are you happy when you're sad? It sounds contradictory. But Jesus said that you are happy when you are mourning. Why? Well, because then you can learn about a source of comfort which is otherwise so incredible, so beyond human experience that no human being can give it to you. But you can have it at that point, and at no other place. "Blessed are they that mourn, for they shall be comforted. Blessed are the meek, for they shall inherit the earth" (Matt. 5:4). He goes on saying these radical, transforming things, and we listen to them and recite them and say that they are wonderful words, but we never take them seriously. Yet what Paul is saying is that these healing, unifying principles revealed in Christ will transform lives. Do you live by those principles? Or do you live by the world's interpretation of them?

J. B. Phillips, in his book *When God Was Man*, gives the usual parody of the Beatitudes:

Happy are the pushers, for they get on in the world.

Happy are the hard-boiled, for they never let life hurt them.
Happy are they who complain, for they get their own way in
the end.
Happy are the blasé, for they never worry over their sins.
Happy are the slave drivers, for they get results.
Happy are the knowledgeable men of the world for they know
their way around.
Happy are the troublemakers, for they make people take notice
of them.

These are exactly contrary to the words of Jesus, but they
truly reflect the way the world lives.

Notice how Jesus, when he is dealing with his disciples,
takes these men of the world, with their conventional approaches, and constantly, gently, and graciously corrects
them. When they are arguing which is the greatest among
them he sets a child in their midst and says, "Look, you'll
never be great until you learn to be like this child. When you
stop trying to be great, when you quit your struggling and manipulating, and in simple, childlike facing of life, trust God,
then you can be great. But you will never make it otherwise."

The mother of James and John comes to him and asks on
behalf of her sons for positions of privilege and favor at his
right and left hand when he comes into his glory. And Jesus
says, "You don't know what you're asking. My kingdom isn't
run that way. No, that position will be given by my Father
to those for whom it is prepared." And he goes on to tell
what prepares us for it: "Unless you drink the cup that I
drink, and are baptized with the baptism with which I'm
going to be baptized, you cannot understand or grasp or have
that kind of position of privilege and favor." He means that
the cross, with its denial, its setting aside of all the old ways,
the way the world operates, and the resurrection, affirming
a wholly new process, a wholly new way of life, resurrection
life will bring you to readiness for privilege and favor. Nothing else will.

In Jesus' parables there are many revelations of a new way
of life, the principles by which the new creation will come
into being. Have you ever wrestled with the parable of the
laborers in the vineyard (see Matt. 20:13–15)? How can

you justify Jesus' words that it was right for the man who owned that vineyard to pay all the laborers the same amount of money, no matter whether they had worked the whole day long or only for an hour? Have you ever struggled with that? Why, the A.F.L. would have shut that vineyard down within ten minutes if they ever heard of anything like that! They would never accept that way of operating. And yet Jesus says that is right. The owner of the vineyard has the right to be gracious above measure to some whom he chooses, and not to others. That is right. But that confounds us, confuses us, bewilders us, baffles us. We don't understand that kind of thinking.

That is what Paul means when he says that this plan which is working out right now in life was set forth *in Christ*. In the wisdom and insight of the Scriptures you will find it, and only there.

The Scriptures reveal a strange thing about Jesus. When you read of his ministry you find that he himself announces that he came to be a peacemaker. He came to heal, to save, to deliver, to liberate. Yet he also said, "I have not come to bring peace, but a sword. For I have come to set a man against his father, and a daughter against her mother, and a daughter-in-law against her mother-in-law; and a man's foes will be those of his own household" (Matt. 10:34–36). The strange thing is that at the beginning, he seems to make things worse rather than better. He increases the division and the strife. He offended the rulers when he spoke. His disciples said to him many times, "Lord, don't you realize that you offended those men? What you said made them angry. You are never going to make it as king if you don't learn how to handle your public relations a little better!" He offended and baffled his own disciples. He hurt them at times by what he said to them. He sent people away instead of trying to get them to join his cause. And it all ended at last in the hurt and heartache and blood of the cross. But out of that hurt and destruction there came ultimate joy and blessing. That is the strange working of God which is set forth "in Christ."

Then Paul looks ahead to the time when the mystery will

be fully manifested. He says it will be "a plan for the fulness of time" (Eph. 1:10a), or literally, "unto the administration of the completeness of the seasons." The seasons that he mentions here are the cycles of history. Any historian will tell you that history moves in cycles. There are times of peace and prosperity which move at last into apathy and lethargy, and this foments disquiet and uncertainty and then finally rebellion and revolution which brings about a change which results in peace and prosperity. You can trace those cycles throughout history again and again and again. Those are what the Bible calls "seasons." Paul says that a time is coming when all these seasons, which have been working incessantly toward a great goal, will be fulfilled—the completeness of the seasons. Someday they will be ended. Then we will know that God has succeeded in tearing down the old creation, destroying it utterly, and at the same time has built up the new.

Tearing Down Is Building Up

This is a remarkable thought that Paul is conveying to us. When I started one summer to build an addition to my home, the first thing we had to do was to tear off part of the roof. (I helped by falling through the ceiling!) The roof had to be destroyed first. We had to destroy the old before we could build the new. But the marvel of God is that he does both at the same time, and by the same process! Do you grasp the implications of that? The heartache, the hurt, the suffering, the injustice, the misery—this is the way he is tearing down the old. But that same heartache and hurt and suffering is the way he is building the new. That is what the Scriptures tell us. That is the amazing revelation, the amazing thought of God which is revealed here. We have references all the way through Scripture to our part in this; we are called upon not only to believe in Christ and follow him, but also to suffer for his name's sake as part of the process. God is doing both at once. By means of the hate and the hurt and the suffering he is building the new creation. And when the old is destroyed, the new emerges at the same time, all finished, complete. That will be "the administration of the fulness of time."

What is our part? Paul has put it in one phrase: ". . . we who first hoped in Christ have been destined and appointed to live for the praise of his glory" (Eph. 1:12). That is our part. This translation softens it to such a degree that we miss a bit of what is said. What Paul literally says is, "We have been made his inheritance." We saints are the inheritance of Christ, his heritage. In verse 18 of this same chapter Paul refers to "the riches of his glorious inheritance in the saints." It is necessary to understand what that means. There is a double inheritance in the Christian life. We inherit Jesus. He is our inheritance. He is our resource from which we draw. If you receive an inheritance you live on it; you use your inheritance to enrich yourself. So Jesus is our inheritance. We can enrich ourselves with him at any moment. He is our power, our strength, our love, our life, our wisdom, our truth. He is what we live by. Christ is our life.

But, and this is the wonderful thing, we are *his* inheritance. He draws on us. Our bodies and souls, our full humanity, are to be his to use to manifest the new creation in the midst of the destruction of the old. That is "his inheritance in the saints." That produces riches, not only in our lives but in the lives of others as well, and the world in general—the riches of his glorious inheritance in the saints.

What does that mean in practical terms? Well, that means that you and I must not complain any longer about what life hands us. It is the Father who has made that choice. He has chosen to put us where we are, and to give us the problems we have, in order that, in the hurt and the heartache and the suffering, and in the joy and the blessing and the riches, whatever they may be, the life of Jesus may be released in that situation. By that means he destroys the old and brings in the new. And as we make ourselves available to him moment by moment—in the shop, in the office, in the home, in the backyard, wherever we are—and as we respond with joy and love and acceptance to the situation in which we find ourselves, God is glorified. Christ receives his inheritance. He finds riches of delight and enjoyment in that. The old is torn down, and the new is built in its place, all in one great, tremendous operation.

Opportunity for Love

I don't fully understand that, but I know it works. I know that is the way God is working. I know, therefore, there is no escape from the heartache and hurt and suffering. It is going to be there for us. But it is an opportunity, never an obstacle!

Let me give you an illustration: Some time ago in my mail I received a thick envelope from the City of Palo Alto, where Peninsula Bible Church is located. In it I found a letter enclosing a petition signed by 114 people who live right near the church, asking the city to revoke our use permit and to restrict our operations as a church.

My first reaction was anger. Why should they do this? Why should they try to stop what is happening here, what God is doing among us? Why should this resistance and opposition arise? I was resentful and defensive. Didn't they know what was happening in terms of changed lives? Didn't they understand that youths were being redirected, and older people revitalized, that homes were being blessed and marriages saved, that life was coming alive in new ways as never before to scores and hundreds of people?

But, of course, I soon realized that they didn't know that. Most of them, probably, had never been inside; only outside. And they were upset. They were annoyed by people who park in such a way as to block their driveways. They were fed up with exhaust fumes because it takes so long for us to get out of our crowded parking lot. They had had enough of noise at night, and of lights that shine into their homes in the middle of the night, and a lot of other things which may seem small to us but which to them were irritations and aggravations.

And then I began to see what this was about. This was God's opportunity given to us to demonstrate a genuine, loving spirit of appreciation and thoughtfulness to our neighbors. This was his opportunity for us to say we're sorry for hurt we've caused, unwittingly to be sure, but inconvenience and annoyance and irritation nevertheless, and for us to respond not in defensiveness but in love; to curtail the annoyances as much as possible, to return good for evil, to invite them to come and see what was happening, and to welcome them to share with us the joys as well as the irritations of what goes on. And, I could pray that our response would be received by our neighbors in a spirit of relief and acceptance.

I had said to myself, at first, "Why should this intervene? Why do we have to take time out to deal with these petty little problems?" But of course the answer is that these aren't petty problems. They constitute a great opportunity, a glorious chance, in this case, to know our neighbors, to break down barriers that we, unknowingly, had erected. It was a chance for the whole congregation to show some love and understanding, and to be extra careful not to annoy those around us, and to apologize when we have, and to renew relationships with these people whom God loves. That is why God sent it. And in the process he will bring in the new, and break down the old.

Our heavenly Father, we are grateful that these great concepts we read about in your Word are not meant merely to delight our intellect; they are meant to guide our lives, to change us, to make us different people. We pray that they will. We pray that what we have learned here about our part in your program—that we are to be available instruments for you to work out your purpose right where we are—may help us to see what look like obstacles and difficulties to be those very opportunities sent our way. And may we realize that you are with us, that you intend to bring it out right, that you will supply the power and strength we need to do it, and that it is all available in Jesus Christ. Help us then to rejoice, Lord, to lift up our heads and be glad, because as we see the old collapsing it is to remind us of the certainty that the new is arising, and that your purpose is being fulfilled. We pray in Jesus' name, Amen.

5

THE WORD AND THE SPIRIT

Ephesians 1:13–14

It is so important that we understand what God is doing! The theme of this whole passage is that God is at work. And it is important that we understand that the universe runs according to the laws of God, not according to the laws of men. Our legislatures enact laws, statesmen negotiate treaties, and we have all the machinery of government to carry them out—and it is right that this should be. But the one factor which is fundamental, which man cannot change, which always keeps on operating exactly as it was intended, is this set of basic laws of the universe which God has set into being. Therefore it is absolutely essential that we find out what God is doing today, and where we all fit into the scheme of God's activity.

So far in this passage we have seen the three-fold God at work. The Father, before the foundation of the world, chose us, called us—those of us who have come to know Jesus Christ as Lord—to be part of his family. What a fascinating concept that is to remember—to remind yourself that God has thought of you, called you, drawn you, appealed to your will, and has made you to be part of his family.

Then we have seen how the Son has liberated us in his death. We have received the forgiveness of our sins—not once, not merely at the beginning of our Christian experience, but again and again and again. Day by day we are experiencing the forgiveness of our failures so that we can live without condemnation, without a sense of guilt, accepted by God. And we are constantly acknowledging those failures, bringing them to him, and going on from there forgiven. Thus, as Paul has put it, he has lavished his grace upon us again and again.

But then, in his resurrection, the Son of God is also at work to break down the barriers in our hearts and lives, until at last, as the Scriptures predict, the new creation will be complete. All things will be united under the headship of Jesus Christ our Lord. What God is doing in Christ is the only thing that will last, and the part we have in that is the only part of our life which is worthwhile.

Now we come to the work of the Holy Spirit. Paul states this clearly for us in Ephesians 1:13–14:

> In him [Christ] you also, who have heard the word of truth, the gospel of your salvation, and have believed in him, were sealed with the promised Holy Spirit, which is the guarantee of our inheritance until we acquire possession of it, to the praise of his glory.

Two things are emphasized here which are always found together in Scripture—the Word and the Spirit. Both are absolutely essential. There is no salvation without both of these. These are the instruments by which God performs his work.

For Balance and Sanity

It is always a mistake to emphasize one of these to the exclusion of the other as some groups today are doing. Some say, "We don't need the Word. All we need is the Spirit's guidance within. All we need is simply to trust the feelings we have. God the Spirit is dwelling in us and he will lead us." But whenever a group does that they follow the pattern of similar groups in the past which invariably results in impractical ideas, mysticism, fanaticism, rigid determinism, and individualism—everybody going his own way and doing his own thing. Utter confusion results if you set aside the Word and try to follow only the Spirit.

On the other hand there are those who try to follow the Word alone. There are many churches today which have lost the freshness and vitality of the Spirit and have been reduced to mechanical, perfunctory performance of the Word. They may be orthodox to the core, but there is no life; they are sterile and dull and lifeless. In dry, mechanical services, they go through a certain form, a ritual observance, and the people go home deadened and dried up. Such people develop a kind of clenched-teeth piety in which they resolve to "do their duty" as Christians, but there is no motivation, no hunger, no satisfaction, no love, no warmth, no joy, no life.

But in Scripture you always find the two together. The Word is interpreted by the Spirit and becomes fresh and vital as the Spirit makes Jesus Christ step out of the pages and stand in your presence in living flesh. You feel the heartbeat of the human Lord who walked here on earth. It is the work of the Spirit to do that. You should never come to the Bible without asking him to take the words and make them come alive. Remember that Jesus appeared to his two disciples on the road to Emmaus and took the Scriptures, the account says, and "beginning with Moses and all the prophets, he interpreted to them in all the scriptures the things concerning himself" (Luke 24:27). As they reported the experience later they said, "Did not our hearts burn within us?" (Luke 24:32). That burning of heart as we read the Word is the work of the Spirit of God, taking the Word and making it alive and vital.

But on the other hand, the Holy Spirit is identified by the Word. There are many spirits abroad today, many voices talking to us, many sources from which information and ideas and solutions to our problems are thrown at us. How do you know which is right? How do you know that it is not the voice of the enemy, cleverly concealed, sounding like the voice of God, appearing to offer you blessing? How can you tell? Only by the Word. It is the Word that identifies the Holy Spirit, and false spirits are detected by this Word. So we must have the Word and the Spirit together for balance and sanity in our Christian lives.

As you look at this passage you can see three things that the Apostle says are normative for Christians. Every Christian who reads this letter can expect to have in his experience these three things which are fundamental to his Christian faith. First, you "have heard the word of truth"; second, you "have believed in him [Christ]"; and third, you "were sealed with the promised Holy Spirit." Those three are essential experiences if you have come to know Jesus Christ.

The End of Illusion

Now let's look at them in more detail. Paul says, "You have heard the word of truth." The world in which Paul lived and wrote was a world like ours today—filled with all kinds of twisted, distorted ideas, with wrong attitudes, with approaches and philosophies which were absolutely flawed and would lead people astray. But people were believing them, as they believe them today. There are many delusions and illusions abroad. We are brought up with our minds cluttered with all sorts of erroneous ideas. How are we ever supposed to keep them straight? Well, the great thing about the gospel is that when you hear this glorious message about Jesus Christ —who he was, the kind of a world into which he came, the reason he came, what he did when he came—you discover that you are listening for the first time to pure, unadulterated truth.

The gospel is regarded by the world in many ways. Some people think of it as one remedy for certain ills, among many possible choices. Some think of it as wishful thinking on the part of the weak and insecure who need something to bolster their morale. Others feel that it is all an illusion or a pipe dream. The communists, for example, say that the gospel is the opiate of the people, that it is fantasy, not real. But the exact opposite is true. The gospel is a return to reality. It is the end of illusion. It is the tearing away of all mistaken concepts and ideas, and it is a return to stark, naked, unadorned fact. The great thing about the gospel is that it puts you back in touch with reality. You begin once again to see things the way they really exist.

Only the gospel describes the true condition of men. Have you ever noticed how easy it is to think about yourself as though there were really nothing very seriously wrong? We all tend to minimize our problems. We think that all we need is to clear up a few areas which are slightly discolored—nothing very serious—just to get rid of a couple of bad habits or to add a bit more morality or to make a stronger effort toward brotherhood or toward more sincerity and courtesy. Then our problems as human beings will be solved. Then we can live together peaceably; we can work out our family struggles and our other relationships. Most people think that way. There is something inherent in us which makes us think that ours is not a very serious problem.

But the gospel shows us that is all wrong. The truth is that we are all murderers at heart. There isn't one of us, if given sufficient motive or an overwhelming period of stress, and under the proper conditions, who would hesitate the slightest second to take another human life. We are murderers at heart! So deep-seated are our problems that there is nothing we can do about them ourselves. We cannot cure ourselves. We cannot save ourselves.

Some time ago I culled a quotation from a speech by Winston Churchill. He was acquainted with the history of humanity. He was himself a history-maker involved in some of the great, sweeping movements of contemporary experience. This is what he said:

> Certain it is that, while men are gathering knowledge and power with ever increasing speed, their virtues and their wisdom have not shown any notable improvement as the centuries have rolled. Under sufficient stress—starvation, terror, war-like passion, or even cold intellectual frenzy—the modern man we know so well will do the most terrible deeds, and his modern woman will back him up!

That is Churchill's analysis of human life.

And that is also what the gospel says. It tells us why we

constantly experience frustration in our lives, why we can't make things go together the way they should. It is because we are experiencing what Scripture calls "the wrath of God." *Wrath* means the removal of restraint. God has taken the bounds off human evil and is allowing it to run its course, to have its head. Consequently we are always being undercut and sabotaged; something goes wrong with all our plans for working things out, a monkey wrench is always thrown into the machinery. This is why we experience bondage. We can't seem to make ourselves do what we want to do, the right thing to do. It is the gospel which tells us why.

Also, it declares God's love for us. It says that God has not forgotten us. It says that he entered human life to share in its sorrow and its pain and, more than that, he went out and personally bore the penalty for our evil in deep, dark, awful mystery—far beyond our imagining and our reasoning—in order that we might have pardon and deliverance and freedom as children of God. All that is in the gospel. That is why it is called "the word of truth." What good news it is—the gospel of salvation!

The second thing the Apostle says is, "Not only have you heard the word of truth and learned the facts about life but, further, you have believed in him." He stresses this, and I would like to stress it too. It is obvious that not only must we hear the word of truth but we must act on it. We must believe it. To believe it means to accept it as truth and to act accordingly. You have never believed unless something is changed in your experience. If you say that you hold something to be true but you go on living exactly as though it were not, then you haven't really believed it. You are only kidding yourself. Belief results in change, in an adjustment to the facts, in conformity to reality. It means that you do something, you take the proper steps in relationship to that which has been revealed to you and which you now see to be true.

Don't Believe in the Gospel

But you will notice that Paul does not specify belief in "it," but belief "in him." We are not to believe in the gospel;

we are to believe in the Lord Jesus. More is required of us than to simply admit the intellectual truth of the plan of salvation. Many people today feel that if you explain the plan of salvation to somebody and he says, "I believe it," he has become a Christian. That is not so. You can believe the plan of salvation and even write theological treatises on it without ever being changed. That is not what changes you. The gospel is not the Savior, it is the Lord Jesus who saves, and he alone. So faith, for a Christian, is always related to a Person, and it involves a personal commitment, a personal relationship. It is never merely an intellectual process nor a belief in a statement of fact.

The apostles never let us forget this. In the first fourteen verses of this very chapter the Apostle Paul mentions the Lord Jesus Christ fifteen times. He is constantly bringing him before us because God wants to drive this great fact home to our hearts. There is no way that you can have blessing from God apart from a continuing personal relationship with the Lord Jesus Christ. We must learn not to believe these people who claim that they are going directly to God; they are only deceiving themselves. It all comes through Christ and by means of a relationship to him.

I remember a dear old Chinese-American lady who came up to me after I had spoken at a Bible conference and asked for an appointment later that day. She insisted upon talking privately, so we got together and she told me her story. She was a medical doctor, had been practicing in that area for more than forty years, and had gained great respect. For forty years she had been attending a certain denominational church. She had tried to discover the truth of Christianity, had joined the church, and was a regular member. But she said that her life was appallingly empty; she was constantly filled with anxiety and fear and a tremendous sense of purposelessness. Finally, in the last year or so, she had resorted to taking Demerol shots in order to quiet her nerves. But this only increased her anxiety and guilt, and she was now almost on the verge of a breakdown. She said that she had gone to her pastor and told him the problem, but after listening to her he had sent her home, saying, "You are just feeling sorry for yourself; that's all."

As we talked, it became apparent to me that in all these years of earnest searching she had never come to a personal knowledge of the Lord Jesus, had never related to *him*. And so I explained to her very simply the invitation he offers: "Behold, I stand at the door and knock; if any one hears my voice and opens the door, I will come in to him" (Rev. 3:20). I asked her to respond to that invitation. Very quietly, without another word from me, she bowed her head and began, almost inaudibly, to pray. I could catch only phrases. She was telling the Lord how empty her life was, how lonely and despairing she had been, how guilty she felt about the drug shots she was taking to alleviate her agony. She simply responded to Jesus' promise and asked him to come into her life. When she finished, I prayed briefly. Then she looked up at me and said, "Oh, thank you so much!" She took my hand and held it and said, "I just can't tell you how much this means to me. Already things are different!" After I had explained a bit more of what the Lord would do for her she turned to me and, with her face just radiant, said, "You know, for the first time in years my stomachache is gone!" Well, that is what it is all about. It is a personal relationship. It is believing in him—not in it, but in *him*.

Guarantee of Redemption

The third thing that the Apostle brings before us here is the strange phrase, "sealed with the promised Holy Spirit." What does it mean to be sealed with the Spirit? Undoubtedly this is a reference to the ancient practice of sealing letters or other objects with sealing wax and impressing the wax with a seal worn on a ring and bearing an identifying image. The use of the seal involved two specific ideas. The first was ownership. The letter belonged to the individual who owned the seal.

That is what Paul is saying here. God sent the Holy Spirit into your life to mark the fact that you belong to him. "You are not your own; you were bought with a price" (1 Cor.

6:20). The presence of the Spirit is your witness that you belong to him. As Paul says in Romans 8, "It is the Spirit himself bearing witness with our spirit that we are children of God" (v. 16). And furthermore, the joy and the peace and the love which he gives to you are a witness to others. As that joy and love and peace begin to flow out through you and spill over into the lives of others, it is a witness. When you begin to love when you don't feel like loving, be joyful when your circumstances are unhappy, be at peace when everything around you is troubled, it is a witness, an unmistakable mark to the world around, that you belong to God. There is something about you that is different. The mark of his ownership is upon you.

The second idea involved in the use of the seal was that of preservation. You remember that the tomb of Jesus was sealed with the seal of the Roman emperor. That seal was intended to keep the tomb inviolate. No one dared break the seal of the emperor upon pain of death. Thus it served to keep the tomb intact, without intrusion or destruction. This is the idea of the Spirit's presence in our lives. It means that God will keep us; as Paul puts it here, he guarantees our inheritance. Something more is to come and it is the Spirit himself who is the guarantee. In Greek, the word for "guarantee" is *arrabon* and it means "a down payment." We are familiar with that in these days of universal credit. You sign a paper and pay a down payment, and that is the *arrabon*, the guarantee that there is more to come. The presence of the Spirit in your life —the joy and the peace that he gives—is the guarantee that there is more yet to come, much more, much better, in fuller quantity, in greater quality even, than what you have experienced so far. Just as the satisfied smile on your banker's face when you pay the down payment and sign the paper means that he knows there is more to come, so the presence of the Spirit in your life is an indication that there is far more yet to come. Great and glorious as our earthly experience may be, it is not the end.

But here we need to correct slightly the translation of the Revised Standard Version. It isn't really ". . . which is the guarantee of our inheritance until we acquire possession of it." The original language is, literally, ". . . until the redemption of the walk-around." This is a reference to the custom of buying a piece of ground and then going out and walking around it. When you walked around it, you made it yours. That was the sign to everybody else that you had paid the down payment and that this was now your piece of property.

That is what Paul says that God has done with us. It is not we who are acquiring possession; it is God. It is he who has walked around us, has marked us out and given us the down payment, the earnest, the *arrabon*, that he will come again and claim his purchased possession. That possession is our body. So Paul is referring here to the resurrection of the body, and in that day, he says, God completes the transaction. He comes to claim the whole thing, all for himself. What he has begun, he will accomplish. In contemporary terms, what the Holy Spirit is saying is, "I will never split, and furthermore, I will never cop out on my responsibilities to you. I will complete what I have begun. I will finish what I have started." This is the sign of the Spirit in our lives, the guarantee of our inheritance, for God has sent the Holy Spirit into our lives for that very purpose.

Only by Faith

All this is in fulfillment of a promise once made to Abraham. Paul calls this the "promised" Holy Spirit. And 4000 years ago, 2000 years before Paul's day, God had promised Abraham that he would bless him, and that through him all the nations of the earth would be blessed. That was the promise that God made. It meant that those who exercised the faith of Abraham would receive the Holy Spirit. That is the way you receive the Holy Spirit—by faith. In chapter 3 of Galatians, the Apostle makes that very clear. He says, beginning in verse 6:

Thus Abraham "believed God, and it was reckoned to him as righteousness." So you see that it is men of faith who are the sons of Abraham. And the scripture, foreseeing that God would justify the Gentiles by faith [not just the Jews, all the nations of earth], preached the gospel beforehand to Abraham, saying, "In you shall all the nations be blessed" (Gal. 3:6–8).

Then look at verses 13 and 14: In the course of time . . .

Christ redeemed us from the curse of the law, having become a curse for us—for it is written, "Cursed be every one who hangs on a tree"—that in Christ Jesus the blessing of Abraham might come upon the Gentiles [what blessing?], that we might receive the promise of the Spirit through faith.

How, then, do you receive the Holy Spirit? Not by pleading, not by waiting upon God and expecting a second experience after salvation. It is impossible to have salvation apart from the indwelling Spirit. The Spirit is received by faith in the Lord Jesus. The minute you believe in him, the minute you commit yourself to him in response to his invitation and he enters your life, in that very moment you are indwelt by the Holy Spirit.

The Spirit himself is God's seal. He marks you out, he identifies you as his, he guarantees you that he will perform every word that he has promised—until you stand in his presence absolutely overwhelmed by all that God has done for you, so completely caught up by the marvelous fulfillment of every word of God's promise that you are almost speech-less—but not quite, because you notice how this passage ends: ". . . to the praise of his glory."

This is the third time Paul has used this phrase in the passage. Each of the members of the Godhead—the Father, the Son, and the Holy Spirit—accomplishes his work so perfectly that it always ends up ". . . to the praise of his glory." The end result is that every one of us, standing at last in God's presence, has a heart filled with praise. And it begins now, as the Spirit does his work within us, to the praise of his glory, so that we can't help but sing and glorify God for all that he has done.

Do you ever wake in the morning and say to yourself, "I am

a child of God. I have been forgiven of my sins. I am accepted in God's family. He has marked me out as his own. He has put his Spirit within me, releasing to me the full life of the Lord Jesus Christ. Every power that Jesus himself had in order to perform his life upon earth, I have in him. Therefore I am equipped to handle whatever comes today. I can take whatever life throws at me because I have him and all the fullness of his life"? That is where you find identity. There is no other ground. That is what enables you to handle whatever may come in your life. Let us praise his glory.

Our heavenly Father, how much we thank you for this revelation of life as it really is. This is the way you see things, and what you see is reality. And Lord, we pray that we may see it not just at this moment but repeatedly, again and again, and that we may not look at ourselves as we so frequently do—as being worthless, useless, and compelled to do evil. You have freed us, Lord Jesus. You have forgiven us. You have liberated us to live for the praise of your glory. Lord, help us to do that in this very moment. Help us to understand that these are facts and to reckon upon them, and tomorrow to reckon upon them again, and the next day. Help us to rejoice in the undergirding fact of our life that we have this relationship to you. We ask you to do this so that we might grow strong in the Spirit's strength, by the power of this Word, in Jesus' name, Amen.

6

TURNED ON BY PRAYER

Ephesians 1:15–18

With verse 15 of Ephesians 1 we leave the great doctrinal passage in which the Apostle Paul teaches the facts underlying our Christian faith and we turn now to his prayer. This study will be a helpful revelation of the place of prayer in the Christian experience—especially in believers who are maturing—and its place in the study of Scripture. Through an understanding of this passage, prayer and the Scriptures are brought together. The Apostle, having set forth what the three-fold God is doing for us, now adds these words addressed to the Ephesian Christians:

> For this reason, because I have heard of your faith in the Lord Jesus and your love toward all the saints, I do not cease to give thanks for you, remembering you in my prayers, that the God of our Lord Jesus Christ, the Father of glory, may give you a spirit of wisdom and of revelation in the knowledge of him, having the eyes of your hearts enlightened . . . (Eph. 1: 15–18).

We will stop there for the time being. I want to call your attention to the reason the Apostle prayed for these Christians. He starts with the words: "For this reason," and then makes note of the evidence which makes him confident they are Christians. The phrase "For this reason" looks back upon the great passage we have just covered, from verse 3 through verse 14, in which the Apostle has been outlining for us the great, fundamental facts about our faith: our call by the Father, his destining us to be his sons, the redemption and forgiveness available to us in the Son, the opening of our eyes to the whole plan of God, our sealing by the Spirit, and his guarantee that we will inherit all that God has provided for us. Paul prays for the saints at Ephesus and others who read this letter because they need to understand these truths.

Convincing Evidence

He is convinced that they are Christians because of two things which have come to his attention—their faith, and their love. That is most instructive. The Apostle evidently has heard in Rome of the faith of these Christians, many of whom were in cities around Ephesus and whom he had never met. He has heard that they have confessed Christ and turned from their pagan idols. They have acknowledged that Jesus Christ is Lord, and have taken open positions as Christians. But what convinced him their faith was true was the evidence of their love—faith that works by love. Because love was beginning to be shown among them, love for all the saints, he knew that the faith they exercised was genuine.

That is very helpful to know, because if your faith has not resulted in your becoming a more loving person, at least in growth in this direction, then it is not genuine faith. It is merely an intellectual acceptance, which means nothing. Remember how James stresses this very fact. He says that faith is revealed by the concern that it awakens for the hungry, the homeless, the needy, and the heartbroken, and our willingness to reach out to heal the hurts of those in society around us. He says, in effect, "Show me your love, and I'll see your faith; but don't talk to me about faith unless love is present." And Paul agrees. He has heard of their love, and so he is aware that their faith is genuine.

And notice that it is love toward *all* the saints, not just toward some of them. Some saints are easy to love. Some are beautiful people, joyful and happy, and everybody likes to be around them. But Paul is struck by the fact that these Christians love all the saints, and therefore their love is not based upon people's personalities, nor upon their wealth; rather, it is based upon the fact that they are saints, they belong to the Lord Jesus, they are in the family of God. This is what every family must learn. If you want harmony in your home you must learn to love your brothers and sisters. They may not be always the most pleasant people, but they are your family. This family love among the Christians in Ephesus is what convinces the Apostle.

Today also, one of the most remarkable signs that a person has genuine faith is that he loves anyone who loves the Lord Jesus. It doesn't make any difference what the person might be like. Sometimes it seems difficult to get Christians to really love one another. They resist opening up to each other and bearing one another's burdens. They have been taught and trained somehow to live in isolation from each other, keeping clear of involvements with anyone else. (That is the way the world lives today.) But such isolationism is always a sign that faith has diminished. If your faith in Jesus Christ is genuine, it always results in love.

Those two qualities, then, have convinced the Apostle Paul that these Christians are real. Therefore, as Christians, they need to know and grasp the great truths he has outlined for them, and it is for this reason that he prays. The important point here is that the command of truth, the knowledge of doctrine, is never enough to enable one to grow up as a Christian. You can learn all that there is in the Bible, and be able to write a very profound and scholarly theological treatise on it, but if it hasn't reached your heart it is absolutely worthless. Truth known never changes anybody; it is truth done, truth which has flowed through the emotions and gripped them and thus motivated the will to obedience.

Thus this passage beautifully takes into consideration the way God has designed us. He has made us so that truth hits the mind first of all, just as it should; we ought to be exposed to the facts, as Paul has expounded them here. But that is never enough. There are people today who think that if you merely study your Bible and take the right courses and learn the doctrine and truth of the Scriptures, that is all you need. But the Apostle makes it very clear that that is never enough. Truth must somehow move from the head down to the heart. It must open "the eyes of the heart," to use the beautiful figure Paul employs. The emotions must be moved, so that the whole man gets involved. He is talking about motivation of the will here, for this wise Apostle knew that nobody ever gets motivated by truth alone. Truth can be dull and academic, so he prays that their hearts might be stirred by the truth.

The Dimension of Prayer

It is prayer that will do that. I have been greatly moved by this passage because it has made me aware that we must add, deliberately and intelligently, the dimension of prayer to our teaching. Teaching truth is never enough. We can teach another person—a student in the Sunday School or our own children at home—so that they can parrot the truth back to us, and we are often satisfied by that. But the Apostle was not satisfied. He knew that you don't *know* truth in that way. You never know it until it has gripped you, and you have been changed by it.

Next, notice the One to whom he prays. He uses two unusual names for God: "the God of our Lord Jesus Christ, the Father of glory." Why does he call him that? Of course God was "the God of our Lord Jesus Christ" when Jesus was here as a man. There is no recognition, here, of the fact that the Son is equal with the Father. Paul does not pray directly to Christ; he prays to the God of the Lord Jesus. That is amazing when you think about it. Why does he do so? Well, the reason is that the evidence we have that God will answer this kind of prayer is that he is the One to whom the Lord Jesus prayed. He is the One upon whom Jesus depended for the enlightenment of his own disciples. For he, too, could not merely teach them and thus deliver them from evil. He had to pray for them in order that the truth might grip their hearts and they might be changed by the truth they knew.

That is why our Lord prayed so often for his disciples, why he spent whole nights on a mountainside, at times, praying truth into his disciples' hearts.

Do you remember when Peter came to him with confidence, with strutting boldness, and told him, "Lord, don't worry about me, I'll never leave you. These other rascals will defect and run away, but you can count on me, Lord. I'll stick with you." Do you remember the Lord's answer to that? "Peter, Satan demanded to have you, that he might sift you like wheat" [that he might run you through a sifter so all the phoniness will be made visible] (Luke 22:31). And Jesus implied by that, "I'm going to give you to him, I'll let him have you." Yet he went on to say, "But I have prayed for you that your faith may not fail" (Luke 22:32). It was that prayer which held Peter together when, three times in one night, he denied his Lord. Finally, gripped by the awfulness of what he had done, he went out and wept bitterly in the streets of Jerusalem. Yet something held him steady. It was the prayer of the Lord Jesus, the power of that prayer which gripped his heart and held him on course. The very God to whom Jesus himself prayed, and upon whom he depended to keep his disciples in the truth that they were learning, is the God to whom we are to pray, that he may open our hearts and lives.

I love the phrase "the Father of glory." There is a lot of hope in that! Do you know what it means? It could mean, of course, "the glorious Father, the Father who is himself glorious." And God is glorious. But I think that here it means, "the One who originates glory, the One who begets glory, the Father who produces it." I attended a wedding reception some time ago, and what a glorious occasion it was! Everyone was joyful and happy, rejoicing with the young couple. It was in a beautiful setting, there was a scrumptious spread of food, and the decorations made it a lovely place. I circulated around, and off in the corner I found a man standing by himself. I talked with him and discovered he was the father of the bride. He had been paying all the bills, and as father of the bride he was the father of the glory. He had produced the glory of this occasion. This is the idea conveyed by that title "the Father of glory." When you pray to God about understanding truth you are asking him to make this truth glorious, to make it come alive, to make it vivid, living, vital. That is what he promises and is able to do. That is why Paul uses that title here; the God to whom Jesus prayed is also the Father of glory, able to produce glory.

Paul turns now and prays for these Christians. Notice what he prays for: ". . . [that he] may give you a spirit of wisdom and revelation in the knowledge of him . . ." (Eph. 1:17b). Why does he say that? Aren't these Christians? Haven't they already been indwelt by the Holy Spirit? Yes. Paul has already acknowledged that. He has said that they were sealed with the Holy Spirit of promise. So he is not praying that they will be given the Holy Spirit. He is praying for a special ministry of the Holy Spirit. In the book of Isaiah, the prophet speaks of the seven spirits of God—the spirit of wisdom, the spirit of understanding, the spirit of counsel, the spirit of knowledge, etc. (Isa. 11:2). He doesn't mean that there are seven Holy Spirits; he means that there is one Holy Spirit who has a seven-fold ministry of illuminating and enlightening the heart. That is what Paul is praying for here, "that he (God) may give you a spirit of wisdom and revelation. . . ."

The Importance of Asking

Notice that he doesn't take it for granted that this will happen. This is not an automatic feature of the Christian life. If you want the Scriptures, the Word of God, the truth, to come alive to you, you must ask for illumination. That is what this passage teaches us. And if you want it to come alive to someone else you must ask that they be given the spirit of wisdom and of revelation. Remember that James says, "You have not, because you ask not." Everything that God has is for us, but it won't be given automatically. Any wise father knows that you can't give to your children in that way. If you were to anticipate all your children's wishes and were always to have whatever they needed ready for them, even before they became aware that they needed it, they would soon take it all for granted. They would fail to develop a thankful spirit. They would fail to develop any sense of need in their lives. No wise parent does that. You learn to wait until your children sense some need, until they come and ask you for help, or until they realize that they are up against it and that there is no other way it can be provided. That is the time to step in. And God does that. He is teaching and training us, and so he allows the Scriptures to remain dull and flat until we ask him to make them glorious.

For all of us a time comes when the Bible becomes dull. We read it and it doesn't say anything, there is no illumination; or we listen to a message and it falls flat; other people seem to be blessed, but we get nothing out of it. What is the reason? Well, it is part of the great conflict which Paul speaks of in the last chapter of this letter—the blinding, hardening, darkening work of the powers of darkness which keeps us from grasping the truth. To counteract that there must be the ministry of prayer, of asking God for a spirit of wisdom and revelation, so that the truth may come alive for us.

I wonder sometimes if much of our teaching doesn't fall flat and much of the training of our children isn't a failure because we have never prayed this for them. Notice how the Apostle is concerned that these mighty truths should be more than mere sentences on the page, that will really grip the lives and hearts of these Christians. Notice also that it is wisdom and revelation "in the knowledge of him" for which Paul prays. Truth finally leads to the understanding of the Person of God.

Into His Presence

Do you pray like that when you read your Bible? Do you open the page and say, "Lord, show me yourself"? This is not merely a book to read in order to learn what is going to happen as prophecy is fulfilled. It isn't merely a book from which to get certain ethical guidelines on how to behave in the relationships of life. Primarily and supremely, this book is designed to lead you into the presence of the living Christ— to feel him, to know him, to sense his love, his wisdom, his strength, his might, his incredible grasp of circumstances, his control of human events. It is to enable you to understand your relationship to him, to have him stand in your presence —living, breathing, compassionate. That is what the Bible is for. That is the wonder of it. No other book has that quality, but this one has. Christ can step out of the pages and be a living presence in your life and heart, if you pray and ask him to give you that spirit of wisdom and of revelation. It will not come in any other way.

If your Bible study time is dull and dreary, take this hint and begin to pray that it might come alive, that you may know him. Remember what Jesus said in his great prayer recorded in the seventeenth chapter of John: "Father, I thank you for our relationship, and I pray that men may know you, the only true God, for this is eternal life." If you want life— life with that quality of abundance which characterizes God —the way to have it is to come to know who God is and what he is like.

Some time ago I read in the China Inland Mission journal an account of two churches among a group of churches in a certain province in the inner part of China. These two churches flourished tremendously, while the others dawdled along at a slow pace. The mission director of that area became very interested in why these two churches were doing so much better than the others. He investigated and found that a couple of years earlier, at a conference in England, information had been given out regarding all these churches, and certain individuals had been requested to pray for the churches. One man took these two churches upon his heart and remained steadfast. Every week he had been praying faithfully for the Christians in these churches, that the truths they heard would be understood. The result was that these churches were like flowers with abundant sunshine and rain. They grew bountifully, while in the other churches the same truth was being taught but no one seemed to grasp it and lay hold of it. This was tremendous testimony to the fact that prayer has power to open eyes.

Now look at the last thing the Apostle says in this introduction to prayer: ". . . having the eyes of your hearts enlightened . . ." (Eph. 1:18). That's a strange expression, isn't it: "the eyes of the heart." We know how expressive eyes can be. A person's face may seem dull and impassive, a "poker" face, but if you look at the eyes you can see something happening within. I have often visited people in the hospital whose faces and whole bodies are wasted away, but whose eyes speak volumes. Eyes are extremely expressive. They are the instrument by which we perceive, by which we see things.

But the mind also has eyes. If you listen to truth in any area or if you study a subject in a book, your mind is perceiving. The eyes of your mind are grasping ideas. But the Apostle tells us here that not only does the mind have eyes, but the heart does as well. The heart also can see things, can grasp truth and understand it. The heart is used in Scripture as the seat of our emotions.

In other words, God is concerned with what the present generation has so beautifully rediscovered for us: that we consist of more than mere minds; that we need also to have our emotions stirred, caught up and captivated by truth. Truth must come first to the mind, then to the heart. The will is never properly motivated until the heart has been moved as well. The whole man must respond to the truth of God. When that happens, then a deep-seated certainty results. You will *know* something with certainty when both the mind and the heart have been touched.

Hearts Burn

We have referred earlier to the episode Luke records for us in his twenty-fourth chapter—the walk to Emmaus when the risen Lord appears to those two disciples. They are defeated, downcast by the horrible thing that has happened in Jerusalem. The Lord joins them, but they don't know who he is. He walks along with them as a stranger and unfolds to them the passages in the Old Testament Scriptures concerning the promised Messiah, including his sufferings and his resurrection. Remember what they said afterward as they were discussing this. They said to one another, "Did not our hearts burn within us while he talked to us on the road, while he opened to us the scriptures?" (Luke 24:32).

That "burning of heart" represents the eyes of the heart being opened. It is the enlightenment, the inflaming of the heart, so that it is deeply stirred and moved. It is this burning of heart that the Apostle desires for these Christians. When the heart begins to burn with truth, when truth from the Word of God becomes vivid and real to you, when it takes root in you and you simply must respond to it, that is when you know with certainty that God is real, that the hope of your calling is genuine, that the power of his presence is available, and that the riches of his ministry through you is manifest to others as well.

I could illustrate this in many ways. I remember an incident that occurred some time ago at our church. A young man became a Christian, came into the church, and married a girl who had grown up in this church. At first his Christian life was glorious to behold. He was warm, open, responsive, and eagerly read the Scriptures. But after a while it all began to ebb away, as often happens. Many Christians go through this experience. He turned cold, lost his interest in the Scriptures, and quit coming to church. He was no longer interested in fellowship with other believers and he avoided them. To use the term of a generation ago, he "backslid."

Naturally, his wife became very concerned. So she and a friend decided they would pray together for her husband every day. She decided in her heart that she would not nag him nor plague him nor push him. She wouldn't urge him to come to church, and thus pressure him into conformity because she didn't want him to come if his heart wasn't in it. She resolved simply to pray. She and her friend met daily, but for a month or more nothing happened; he went on pretty much in the same way. But they took the advice of the Lord Jesus: "they [men] ought always to pray and not lose heart" (Luke 18:1), and they kept on praying.

Gradually her husband's attitude began to change a bit. One day she came home and found him reading the Bible.

She didn't say anything to him, and he didn't say anything to
her, but she was encouraged. Then one Sunday he announced
that he was going to church with her. Again she rejoiced inwardly, but didn't make a big deal of it. After a while he
finally said to her, "You know, dear, I've really been way out
of it! Somehow or other I lost all my interest in the Lord.
But God has moved and met me and brought me back." And
he came alive again. What a wonderful testimony to the
power of prayer to open eyes!

It isn't enough simply to teach truth. It isn't enough to
spread doctrine. It isn't enough to have a Bible class in which
you are getting the students to learn certain facts from the
Scriptures. The Apostle Paul and the other great leaders of
the early church understood man much better than that. You
never get the whole man until the heart is moved, until the
eyes of the heart are enlightened, until truth is moved from
the head down to the heart and thus grips the emotions.
Then the will is properly motivated, and the person begins to
grow tremendously.

What an encouragement this is to a ministry of prayer!
Pray for one another. Pray for the class that you teach. Pray
for your children—that the truth they are learning, both at
home and at Sunday School, will become vivid to them. How
many times have we allowed them merely to learn factual
matters, and have never prayed about it, and then wondered
why the truth doesn't seem to affect them very much. Pray for
your father and mother—that the truth they are learning may
change their hearts so that they will be easier to get along
with. Pray for your husband, pray for your wife—that this
enlightenment of the heart may come. See how Paul understands this and how he stresses it with us. He says, "For this
reason"; there is no use teaching you this truth unless I also
pray for you, unless prayer changes your life so that you are
"turned on," so that your hearts come alive with the truth of
God. And if we do the same we will understand that God has
designed truth to make its appeal to the whole of our humanity, the whole being, the whole man, and we will become
whole in Christ.

Our heavenly Father, we thank you so much for this revelation of the way we are made. Thank you for the wisdom of the Apostle Paul, who knew that there must be the bending of the knee, the opening of the heart, the imploring of the Spirit, the bathing of the truth; the Word, in prayer, so that it becomes vital, living, attractive, compelling. Lord, help us to pray for each other. We need this truth greatly today, and we pray that you will drive it home to us with clarity and with power, in Jesus' name, Amen.

7

HOPE, RICHES, AND POWER

Ephesians 1:18–23

Are you remembering my exhortation to read through the book of Ephesians often while we work through these passages together? You will find that your life will never be the same again if you keep reading through this text.

We have now arrived at the last part of the first chapter of Paul's letter. We have learned from him that growth in Christians involves two fundamental requirements. First, the mind must be carefully instructed in the great facts of reality upon which our faith can rest. But that is not enough; there must also be the prayerful enlightenment of the heart. Paul is not content to leave these people merely taught; he also prays that the truth which they have heard and understood with their minds will come alive and capture their hearts with a kind of "divine heartburn."

The Apostle understood these Christians. He was a veteran warrior of the cross. He had been a Christian for many years by the time he wrote this letter and he had undoubtedly gone through all the varying experiences to which a Christian can be subjected. He knew the lukewarmness which can set in, the lethargic, apathetic attitudes which can sometimes arise after a warm and hopeful beginning. He saw these Christians as dispirited, listless, turned off, and he understood their need. Perhaps you are struggling with this very problem. No Christian escapes this entirely in his lifetime.

Because Paul understands this, he turns to prayer, and his prayer reflects his understanding of their needs. He specifies three things. He prays that the eyes of their hearts will be enlightened so that

> . . . you may know what is the hope to which he has called you, what are the riches of his glorious inheritance in the saints, and what is the immeasurable greatness of his power in us who believe . . . (Eph. 1:18–19a).

Hope, riches, and power. You will notice that he doesn't pray in general, as most of us tend to do. He doesn't simply say, "Lord, bless the Ephesians this morning." Paul knows these people better than that. He knows that they have lost their vision. It seems to them as though nothing is happening in their lives and they are going nowhere. They have lost their sense of hope. They know it as a doctrine, but they have lost the experience of it. So Paul prays that God will enlighten their hearts so that they may know the hope of God's calling, the hope to which he has called them.

The Hope of Glory

We all know the need for hope. This word, of course, is one part of the great triad found very frequently in the Scriptures: faith, hope, and love—the essentials to living a full-orbed Christian experience. Hope always concerns the future. These people had obviously lost their sense that anything happening in their lives could affect the future. This happens to many of us; we are all waiting for the coming of the Lord, but it doesn't really turn us on very much. We know it as doctrine, but it isn't very exciting.

The hope of a believer is described for us very plainly in Romans 8:18–25 which we should read so that we will understand what hope he wanted to awaken within their hearts:

> I consider that the sufferings of this present time are not worth comparing with the glory that is to be revealed to us (v. 18).

That is the hope—a glory which is coming, a glory toward which we are moving day by day. That glory is waiting for us, Paul says. It is a glory which touches the whole world:

> For the creation waits with eager longing for the revealing of the sons of God; for the creation was subjected to futility, not of its own will but by the will of him who subjected it in hope; because the creation itself will be set free from its bondage to decay and obtain the glorious liberty of the children of God (vv. 19–21).

That phrase, "the bondage to decay," is a very accurate description of what scientists call the Second Law of Thermodynamics, the law of entropy, the law which states that everything in the universe is running down; it was wound up once, but now everything is declining, deteriorating. Paul includes not only the natural world, with its constant decay, but the human body as well. He says:

> We know that the whole creation has been groaning in travail together until now; and not only the creation, but we ourselves, who have the first fruits of the Spirit, groan inwardly [and sometimes outwardly] as we wait for adoption as sons, the redemption of our bodies. For in this hope we were saved. Now hope that is seen is not hope. For who hopes for what he sees? But if we hope for what we do not see, we wait for it with patience (vv. 22–25).

These believers knew academically that a day was coming when their bodies would be redeemed, that God was working out that transformation, and that a whole new day was ahead. The central factor of this hope is the certainty of a new humanity. And you will notice that this hope is not just a faint possibility. It isn't an uncertain dream lying in the distant future. It is an absolutely guaranteed certainty, toward which we are now moving, that we will one day live in a whole new creation and will be men and women endowed with a spirit which can mount up with wings as the eagle, a

soul that can run and not be weary, a body which can walk
and not faint, equal to the demands of the spirit.

We know how true it is, in the words of our Lord, that the
spirit is often willing, but the flesh is weak. About the best
we can manage to say is that the spirit is willing, but the flesh
is ready for the weekend! We need rest; we look forward to
relaxation. But a day is coming, says God, when we will be in
a new body, which will be equal to all the demands of the
spirit, so that we never get weary or tired. We're looking forward to that day.

It's Happening Now

"Well," you say, "that's fine. I understand that. But how
does that help me now? Now I'm bored, I'm caught up in a
meaningless routine. Day by day goes by and life is not very
exciting. How does that distant hope help me now?" The
answer is that the Scriptures do not teach that this hope is
going to be attained in one blinding flash at the end. I think
many Christians today misunderstand it in this way. Perhaps
these Ephesians did too, and this was their difficulty. What
the Scriptures actually teach about this hope had perhaps
never dawned upon them. The fulfillment will not come at
one moment in the resurrection at the end of life, or at the
end of the age, but it is happening right now. It is true that
the body is ultimately redeemed at that future time, but the
new creation is taking place right now. Read the way Paul
describes it in these most helpful words in 2 Corinthians
4:16–17:

> So we do not lose heart [we don't get discouraged]. Though our
> outer nature is wasting away, our inner nature is being renewed
> every day. For this slight momentary affliction is preparing for
> us [right now!] an eternal weight of glory beyond all compari-
> son. . . .

That is what is happening now! I never read the phrase
"this slight affliction" without thinking of Paul's description
of his own experience a little farther on in that same letter.

He had been beaten with rods three times and had received thirty-nine lashes five times. He had been shipwrecked three times and had been adrift at sea for a night and a day. He had even been stoned once (not on LSD or something like that —rocks had been thrown at him) and left for dead. He was in danger constantly from false brethren, and spent many sleepless nights and many days without food or drink. All this he describes in one phrase: "this slight momentary affliction." And he says that this is working for us, it is preparing us. It is preparing for us an eternal weight of glory beyond all comparison.

Paul prays here that these Christians will capture this sense that God is at work in their daily circumstances, and that in the midst of the old creation the new one is gradually taking shape. You can't see it, although perhaps as you look back you can see some of the results of it in your spirit and in your soul. But these very trials and pressures and problems and afflictions are preparing us for that future time.

That means that the flat tire you had on your car yesterday which upset you so—you discovered it just as you were in a hurry to go some place—is working for you. It is preparing you for this day. It is teaching you something about how to be patient, how to handle your pressures. It is giving you a chance to exercise some of the power of Christ which is available to you. That spot of shoe polish you got on your best dress, the weariness you feel at the end of the day, the arthritic pains in your shoulder, the spat you had with your best friend —all this, you see, is working together for your good. That is the point. That is what Paul wants these Ephesians to see. They are not lost in a meaningless routine of events, drifting through with some degree of numbness day after day. No, it is all working together. It is preparing them for an eternal weight of glory beyond all comparison.

The Touch of Heaven

Learn to look at life that way! That is the hope of our calling. There is no circumstance we go through which cannot, in the hands of God, be turned to our advantage. Granted, we often allow ourselves an immediate failure at that point, but that failure is not the end of the story. We can go back and say, "Lord, I see now that I didn't need to give way to the flesh, to its despair or its reaction of anger or impatience. Thank you for showing me that. When the situation arises again I'll be more ready to rest upon your sustaining grace. I'll be more experienced in how to turn the problem over immediately to your strengthening hand." When you begin to see that, then every moment, every event is tinged with the flame of glory, with the touch of heaven upon it.

Paul knew also of their sense of impoverishment. He knew that these Christians tended to grow dull and flabby in their experience. They had begun with a vast comprehension of the greatness of God and the glory of life, and they had been set free from the habits which had held them in bondage. But now, without realizing it, they were gradually drifting into a narrowness of experience. They were becoming limited and provincial. A sort of living *rigor mortis* was setting in. They were becoming "established." (That usually means inflexible and rigid!) This condition afflicts many Christians.

I heard recently of a large evangelical church, orthodox to the core, where the people were exposed to a great deal of Bible teaching. But the outstanding characteristic of that church was an increasing inflexibility and narrowness. For those people the walls of their lives were moving in, limiting them as to what they could or could not do. They were gradually falling into a rut as they backed away from facing the real issues. They were extremely unappealing and un-attractive to others around, but they seemed to be only dimly aware of it.

Paul is aware of this condition that can afflict any Christian and so he prays that these Ephesians may know "what are the riches of his [God's] glorious inheritance in the saints." Notice how he puts that. He is not asking that they under-stand that God is their inheritance. It is true that God is our resource. He is our strength; we draw upon him. He belongs to us. But what Paul is emphasizing here is that we belong to God. We are his property. He has an inheritance in us. It is his delight to use us. And if we make ourselves available to be used, then enrichment and fulfillment beyond our wildest dreams await us. But if we are afraid to let God use us we will narrow down into this hardened rut of experience, and we will find that the Christian life gradually turns dreary and gray.

Available for Adventure

What is needed is an understanding of the adventure which awaits anyone who makes himself available to God. This is Paul's appeal in Romans 12: "I appeal to you therefore, brethren, . . . to present your bodies as a living sacrifice, . . . unto God" (v. 1). Give him your life day by day, not just in one crisis moment of dedication but in every situation. Say, "Lord, do you want to use me in this situation? Okay, here I am. I'm available. I see this need right in front of me. Help me, Lord, not to pass by on the other side. Give me the grace to be available now. Lord, have you given me gifts? Is there equipment in my spirit that you want to use? Well, here it is, Lord; I'm available for you to use to meet this need." And then move out, venture out, plunge in, risk a little. As you do you will discover that this brings enrichment of life, that your life gradually becomes delightful in its adventure, broad in its understanding, rich in its varied experience.

I once attended a conference at a beautiful estate on the Columbia River. It was a glorious autumn day, and after the morning meetings I wanted a chance to be alone so I took a walk. I was walking along a rather well-defined, wide path, when I saw a little trail wandering off to the side. It looked as if it led down toward the river, and I thought perhaps it might open up a vista of the Columbia River gorge. It was a steep path, and I knew that when I came back up the going might be a little tough, but I decided to try it. I hadn't gone two hundred yards before I broke into a clearing where I had a tremendous, glorious view of the whole river, the gorge, the autumn colors, the cliffs, the mountains beyond. It was well worth taking that path!

I was thinking of this verse as I walked back up that path,

thinking of how Paul prays that we might understand the riches of God's glorious inheritance in the saints, the thrill of being used of God. It struck me that I had just experienced a living parable of that. I had to take the chance that the path went somewhere. It didn't appear to be much of a path, it could have dwindled into nothing, so I had to risk something. But it was well worth the risk, because it enriched my life with the beauty of that scene. And God is speaking in that way to you. Many of you are waiting for God to tell you to do something. But the New Testament never instructs you to wait. Its message is: "God is with you; therefore reach out, risk, venture, plunge in, try something new that you've never done before and trust God to see you through it." The result will be fantastic enrichment of life. That promise awaits anyone who will let God have his inheritance in his life, if he will present his body to him and say, "Lord, here I am, available to you."

There is one final element in Paul's request here: "that you may know . . . what is the immeasurable greatness of his power in us who believe" (Eph. 1:18–19). The Apostle knows that these Ephesian Christians, like Christians everywhere, are often immobilized by the grip of fear. He knows their insecurity. He knows that they are afraid of their neighbors, afraid of failure, afraid of persecution and ridicule. There is a deep sense of inadequacy and impotence in their lives. They don't think they can do anything. They know how entrenched the forces of evil around them are and it seems hopeless to try to challenge any of the social situations of the day. They know what tremendous, relentless pressures the world can bring to bear upon those who seek to change some of these situations, and they are afraid.

The Answer to Fear

The minute you feel a sense of adequate power, you lose fear, because power overcomes fear. Love overcomes fear. These forces are mighty, powerful forces. And so Paul prays that Christians will have their eyes opened, in a practical way, to the power available to them—"that you may know what is the immeasurable greatness of his power in us [not up in heaven somewhere, but in us] who believe." I am often distressed by how easily many Christians seem to give up. They feel that their struggles are too great and they just can't make it. But this sense of defeat is theirs because they have lost sight of the One who is giving them power. Paul develops this at some length here because it is so important to us. He wants us to see that this power was first demonstrated in the resurrection of Jesus:

> . . . according to the working of his great might which he accomplished in Christ when he raised him from the dead and made him sit at his right hand in the heavenly places . . . (Eph. 1:19–20).

It is resurrection power. That means that it is different; it is not like any other power. It isn't the power of a strong personality nor of an educated mind. It isn't the power of a good family background nor of money, numbers, or leadership ability. It is the power that raised Christ from the dead that is able to bring life out of death. What does that mean in practical terms? Well, it means, as I have often said, that it works best in a cemetery. If you are living in a cemetery, if everything is dead and dull and lifeless around you, try resurrection power. That is what it is for. It means that this power takes no notice at all of obstacles, just as Jesus rose from the dead, paying no attention to the stone, to the decrees of Caesar, to the fulminations of the Jewish priests, nor to the guard in front of the tomb. Resurrection power doesn't pay any attention to obstacles. It surges on ahead, leaves the problems to God, and goes on. And resurrection power requires no outside support. It doesn't rely upon someone else, nor upon something else. It doesn't need a vote of confidence. It doesn't require any kind of undergirding expressions of support from anybody. It can operate alone, completely alone, if necessary. And it makes no noise or display. It doesn't try to arrest attention by some publicity stunt. It effects its transformation quietly, bringing life out of death.

One more thing: Notice that the Apostle declares that resurrection power is supreme in the universe:

> . . . far above all rule and authority and power and dominion, and above every name that is named, not only in this age but also in that which is to come . . . (Eph. 1:21).

It is far above, far greater than any other force, stronger than anything which can be launched against you. So believe these words! This is what the Apostle is praying for—that you will really grasp this thought, understand that this is exactly what God means.

God's power is made perfect in weakness. Perhaps your problem is that you are trying to feel strong. You want to feel powerful. But God says, "No, resurrection power is the kind that works best when you feel weak." So if you feel weak, thank God. And the next time you find yourself threatened with temptation, run to Christ in helplessness. Commit yourself to him again. Say, "Lord, I can't handle this myself. I can't control myself. If you don't help me, I'm sunk!"

No Greater Power

Paul says a little farther on that Christ is seated at God's right hand in the heavenly places [i.e., in the seat of power in the universe], far above all rule and authority and power and dominion. Therefore, obviously, if God is at work in you, and if he has that kind of power, then nobody else's power even approaches his. No demonic force, no lustful urge, can be greater than the power of Jesus Christ. When you see that fact, you will be able simply to rest in the Lord, and it will work. God will set you free!

Paul stresses the fact that the name of Jesus is greater than any name that is named. When you name a name you are stating the resource upon which you intend to act. A policeman acts in the name of the law. The President of the United States acts in the name of the people. A salesman acts in the name of the company. And there are men and women today trying to act in the name of Satan. But here is a name which is above every name. Of any name that can be named, the name of Jesus is greater, not only in time but in eternity as well, not only in this age but in the age to come. Never will there be a greater name than the name of Jesus. What encouragement that gives!

Power Made Visible

The last thing Paul tells us of this power is that it is all made visible in the church:

> . . . and he has put all things under his feet and has made him the head over all things for the church, which is his body, the fulness [the manifestation, the visible expression] of him who fills all in all (Eph. 1:22–23).

The only place this kind of power is ever going to be shown is in you and me, in the midst of our pressures and problems—power to be patient (that takes power, doesn't it?), power to love when someone is irritating the socks off you, power to be joyful in the midst of distressing circumstances, power to be thankful. That is what Paul is talking about—power to live as God intended men to live.

At a recent conference, after one of my messages a man came up to me and rather abruptly said, "You know, we're going to have to find some way to shut you up!" I wondered what he was getting at. He said, "If you keep on talking this way, men like me are going to be out of work." I asked, "What do you do?" He said, "I'm a psychiatrist! But seriously, I want you to know that what you are saying, I have recently discovered, is the secret that can make psychiatry work." I found that not too long ago he had become a Christian. Now he was enjoying the discovery of a secret he had puzzled over and wondered at before—why some of the psychiatric techniques he had been taught would work and others wouldn't. Now he understood that a new power is available, and that in that power these psychiatric approaches can be made to work consistently, so he had begun to correct his psychiatry by the Scriptures.

God is telling us here that he has come to give us hope, and riches, and power—power to be what we ourselves want to be.

Our heavenly Father, we ask that the mighty prayer of this great Apostle will become true of us, that we, too, will discover how encouraging it is that our failures are working for us "a far more exceeding and eternal weight of glory," that even in the times when we are distressed and we don't handle the situation rightly, if we will turn back to you, that situation will work out to our advantage. Lord, we thank you for this encouragement that if we will venture even a little, our lives will be enriched thereby. And we are grateful that above all, and undergirding everything else, is this amazing power within us, that is able quietly to bring life out of death, hope out of hopelessness, joy out of sorrow, and beauty out of ashes. Lord, we ask that we will understand this and live by it and act on it, so that the world around will begin to see it in us. We ask in Jesus' name, Amen.

8

THE HUMAN DILEMMA

Ephesians 2:1–3

Perhaps you have already noted in your reading that the great theme of Ephesians is the unifying, restoring work of Jesus Christ. He has come to smash every barrier among men, to span every chasm, to break down every obstacle which divides and fragments humanity, and to unite all things together in himself. The good news of the gospel is that he has already begun.

In the last chapter we looked at Paul's prayer for the Ephesian Christians and noted how he beseeches God that all his readers will grasp the amazing greatness of the power that brings about the restoring work of God in Christ. When you really see the resources made available to us in Christ, and they begin to hit you with the impact they deserve, you will never live in the same way again. So Paul prays that the power of God may be evident to us, the power which breaks through the problems of men and restores harmony and peace and joy in the midst of death.

But you will never understand these problems, as the Apostle goes on to show us in chapter 2, until you grasp the difficulties our Lord faces—the condition of mankind in its lost state—and how absolutely impossible it is for man to do anything to change himself. It takes the great power of God; nothing else will suffice. That is the theme of the first half of chapter 2. In the second half Paul deals with another obstacle which hinders the unifying work of Jesus, and that is the alienation of the Gentiles from the Jews. There was a division in humanity, a sharp and severe cleavage which kept the vast majority of the people on the earth away from the knowledge of God, and Paul shows how this division has been dealt with in Christ.

The Most Difficult Truth

But now, in this first section, Paul takes a look at the condition of man. As you read the first three verses, keep in mind that this is probably the most difficult truth in all of Scripture for human beings to believe. Here at the outset of this section is the revelation of a truth so difficult for us to grasp, and *believe*, that most of us choose to water it down. We don't accept it; we won't believe it. As a consequence we have no realistic outlook on where we are, either on the tremendous hopelessness of our condition if we are without Christ, or on the glory and the wonder of our position if we are in Christ. But if you want to have your heart set on fire, listen carefully to these verses so that we might see what is the immeasurable greatness of his power which has cured this condition.

In the Revised Standard Version the first phrase of chapter 2 is, "And you he made alive. . . ." The translators actually borrowed these words from a little later on in the chapter. Paul doesn't really say that at this point. He is so intent upon getting before the people the description of humanity and its problem that he just runs right on, ignoring grammar and everything else. This is a most ungrammatical sentence in the original Greek. But the translators bring this phrase in here so that we will get the point toward which Paul is driving.

And you he made alive, when you were dead through the trespasses and sins in which you once walked, following the course of this world, following the prince of the power of the air, the spirit that is now at work in the sons of disobedience. Among these we all once lived in the passions of our flesh, following the desires of body and mind, and so we were by nature children of wrath, like the rest of mankind (Eph. 2:1-3).

There is the Apostle's great analysis of the problem. This is the difficulty Jesus Christ faces when he comes to a man or a woman, a boy or a girl. What it takes to break through this condition is nothing less than the immeasurable greatness of his power. What is difficult for us to believe is the summary Paul gives of the general state of man. He says that all mankind is dead, in trespasses and sins.

It is extremely difficult for us to believe that we are dead. If you come to a high school kid who is ready to go out for football, feeling the challenge of a new sport, involved with his friends in all kinds of exciting activities, and looking forward to building a life of his own, and you say, "You're dead," he will look at you with pity in his eyes. "What kind of person are you, some kind of a nut?"

But study Paul's analysis and I think you will see what he means and how accurate this description is. There are two basic characteristics which we immediately associate with a dead person. The first is their utter impotence, their powerlessness.

A friend of mine told me of the time he was taken on a tour of a mortuary by a young Christian man who worked there part time. They came into the room where the bodies were lying out on slabs, and the young man pulled back a sheet and said, "Tell him about Jesus." My friend said, "I've never forgotten that! How impotent is a person who is dead! How impossible it is to reach him. How difficult, how absolutely hopeless it is for him to respond to any appeal, to do anything constructive."

The second mark of death is corruption. The reason mortuaries exist is that dead bodies tend immediately to deteriorate. They decay, they fall apart, they lose their consistency, they begin to rot, to smell. You remember that in the story of Lazarus, Martha said to Jesus, "It's too late, already he stinks. He's been dead four days." That is also a mark of death—corruption. Impotence and corruption.

Right Intentions—Wrong Results

The Apostle suggests that those two conditions are the indications that men without Christ are dead. First he uses the word *trespasses*; they are dead through trespasses. Do you know what a trespass is? This is a word which comes from a basic Greek word which means "to miss your step." If I start to walk downstairs and I aim at the first step, but miss it and come down on another step, that is a trespass. I have misstepped. I didn't intend to; I aimed at the top step and intended to hit it, but I missed it. Though my intention was right, the result of my action was wrong.

This is what Paul says characterizes humanity. We are guilty of missteps. We don't mean to do them, but we end up missing the way. We start out with great ideals, with an image of what we would like to be. We aim at that, we try to be that, but somewhere we miss the mark. We don't fulfill our ideals, we don't realize our dreams. And even when we achieve the things we thought we wanted, we find them to be hollow pleasures indeed, empty and unsatisfying. Many of us suffer from that widespread disease of our day called "destination sickness," the malady of having arrived where you wanted to go, but not liking it when you get there, and remaining unsatisfied. That is the impotence of human life. We cannot fulfill our best ideals. No matter how hard we try, how much we resolve, something keeps us from them. That is a mark of the death which is present in humanity everywhere.

I was in San Diego not long ago with the National Youth Workers Conference. Os Guinness, the brilliant young associate of Dr. Francis Schaeffer, was there. He has written a book containing some very penetrating studies and analyses of present thinking among men. He has read all the books that the thinkers of today are writing about the future, about what is coming and what mankind can do about it. He has noted the polarization which exists in human thought between two extremes. On the one hand, there is pessimism, a stark realism which sees no hope whatsoever for the future beyond a few short years ahead—most of the books are like that—and on the other, a naïve and completely unrealistic optimism, such as is reflected in Huxley's *Brave New World*. Despite all the problems, according to the optimists, we are somehow going to work it all out. The mass of humanity swings desperately back and forth between those two extremes.

As he analyzed each bright, new, promising hope that men of this caliber set forth, he found the fatal flaw in each one—the fact that it would not work, could not work, does not work, has not worked when tried before in history. Gradually, he said, as he studied, an intense depression of spirit came upon him. He felt simply overwhelmed by the emptiness, the hollow mockery, of this kind of perspective. When he put it all together in a book, he chose these words for the title: *The Dust of Death*. But when he came back to the Scriptures and to the resurrection of Jesus it was like a fresh wind blowing through all the dust of humanity's hollow dreams. This is what Paul is saying. There is this well-intentioned, misstepping tendency within man which marks his death.

But beyond that, there are our sins. There are not only the times we fail when we meant to do right, but there are also times when we intentionally and deliberately do wrong. Sin is the violation of truth when we know it to be truth. This is what creates the downward trend, the deterioration of life.

Most of us start in, as I have said, with rather high ideals and wholesome attitudes. We approach life, many of us, with good moral standards because of the homes and training and background we have had. And we are the ones who find it most difficult to believe this passage. Yet all of us can recognize that some of the things we do now with utter disregard and total acceptance horrified us when they were first suggested to us. And even when we first did them we were uneasy of spirit. But now they have become commonplace and we indulge without any difficulty at all. That marks the downward trend, the deteriorating faculty in life. This is a mark of death, a corruption which is increasingly evident as our population explodes, and which produces an awful sense of despair and hopelessness in human society today. How accurate Paul's analysis is when you set it against life. No other philosophy can adequately explain human life.

Now Paul explains what is behind this condition. Why is this so universally true? There are three forces at work, he says. The first is in the words, "following the course of this world." Literally it is, "following the age of this world." The characteristics of our age exert certain pressures on us. We are made to conform by the world in which we live. By *world* Paul is referring to human society—not the earth itself, with its mountains and lakes and trees; that belongs to God—but secular society, trying to live apart from God, determined to work out all its problems without any reference whatsoever to God. That world will produce a tremendous pressure to conform.

Haven't we all felt it? This is why fashions are always so powerfully influential among us. We hardly dare be different. Or if we are different, we break away completely and form another society whose members are made to conform within it. That is why you never see a hippie with a crew cut. They don't like crew cuts. They reject short hair because that is a pattern they have learned to associate with something else they reject. But in the hippie world everybody must have long hair. And if you try to break away from that conformity you will form a new society, a new pattern, in which it is the style, *de rigueur*, to have medium-length hair. In any case, there is always this pressure to conform.

But conformity is involved not only in the realm of fashion, but also in the way we react, in our attitudes. We are governed by the attitudes of our associates, and we are pressured to conform by our peers around us. That is the world, and what tremendous pressure it exerts! How it rejects anybody who is noticeably different! That is why the world hates genuine Christianity. Genuine Christians belong to neither of the extremes which are always present in society. They have to contrast with both. And therefore they are attacked from both sides, if they are really standing where Christ stands. One of the indications of whether or not your Christianity is genuine is whether you do get attacked from both sides, because Christianity is really a third way of life.

The Devil's Commodity

Yet beyond the world, says Paul, lies something else—a sinister being. He calls this force "the prince of the power of

the air, the spirit that is now at work in the sons of disobedience." Do you see how he is taking us back, behind the fa-
cades, behind what we call the normal activities of life? He is
tearing off the veil and revealing to us what is really there. He
says that there is an organized realm of malevolent beings,
headed by a ruler of incredible subtlety and power who is at
work behind the world scene to create disobedience. That is
the devil's stock in trade—disobedience.

Paul calls him "the prince of the power of the air." When
he refers to the air I don't think he means literally the oxy-
gen-nitrogen mixture we breathe, although who knows but
what the devil has in some way twisted the physical atmosphere. I'm a bit tempted to pursue this idea to see what
might be involved in the thought that the very air we breathe
is more than polluted: It is twisted. But this phrase is more
likely a metaphorical reference to the fact that as the air per-
vades our environment and yet is invisible to us, so the devil
and his angels are arrayed against God, surrounding us on
every side, invisible, and yet constantly manipulating the human race. The devil and his demons use the pressures of the
world and, (as we'll see later on) the flesh, to affect the
minds and hearts of men so that they act disobediently.

But you must have something to obey in order to be disobedient. Paul is referring here to disobedience in the face of
the truth. The God of truth is always trying to capture our
attention and to set reality before us, but there is an evil spirit
at work in society which is constantly saying, "When you see
it as truth, don't do it." You can illustrate that in a thousand
ways. It is amazing what a commitment we have to disobedience! This is why we have to have litter laws, for instance. It
should be sufficient merely to point out to people that if you
throw beer cans along the road you will destroy the beauty of
the road. Merely putting up a couple of signs to remind people of that fact ought to be enough. But it isn't. People throw
the cans out and hit the signs which say DON'T LITTER. It is a
mark of a disobedient spirit at work.

This is why our initial reaction to some demand is almost
always, "Why should I? Who do you think you are? Why

should I do what you ask?" Or even if someone politely requests something of us, our first reaction is, "Well, tell me why. I want to know that first." There seems to be a tinge of disobedience about almost everything we do. Why is that? The Apostle says that it is because a disobedient spirit is at work—one who is constantly challenging every single law and force which God has called into being for the good of mankind. He is assaulting us and working through us, constantly trying to get us to be disobedient to the truth that we know.

Now Paul goes further, bringing this right down to the individual. We have looked at society, back of which is the malevolent cruelty and malicious design of the devil. He is a being of incredible power, subtlety, and wisdom, with whom none of us is able in any degree to match wits. He'll trap us every time, as he has all through the history of the world. But what about the individual in society? Paul adds, "Among these we all once lived in the passions of our flesh [literally, the desires of the flesh], following the desires of body and mind . . ." (Eph. 2:3). That brings us right to where we live. The "passions of the flesh" is an individual matter.

Paul uses a word here which is used elsewhere in Scripture many times, both for good and bad. He calls them the *lusts* of the flesh, the passions or the desires of the flesh. The "lusts of the flesh" does not necessarily have a bad connotation. The flesh is our basic human nature. It is the way we human beings are constructed. We live in a body of flesh and bone. But the Scriptures indicate that something has happened to that flesh. Something has gained control of it and has begun to twist it, and Paul shows us in a moment just what that twist is.

But there are also good things about the flesh. That is, there are basic desires of the flesh which God created. Among them are hunger and thirst, the desire for sex, the desire for attention, for acquisition of goods, and the enjoyment of pleasure. There is nothing wrong with them. Jesus used the very word which here is translated "passions" when he said to his disciples in the upper room, "I have earnestly desired to eat this passover with you . . ." (Luke 22:15). Literally,

"With much lust have I lusted to eat this passover with you."
So lust is not always wrong, and the Apostle recognizes that
this is the case. We human beings have normal, natural desires—we want to eat, we want to drink, we want to sleep, we
want to have sex. These are perfectly proper desires.

Passions Gone Wrong

But Paul uses another term here which shows that there is
a twist to them. The satanic treachery comes out at this
point—what is translated here "the desires of the body and of
the mind" is a subdivision of these passions of the flesh. The
word he uses for "desires" is really the word *will*. It carries
with it the thought of an unbreakable resolve, a determination. Perhaps the nearest English equivalent today is the
word *drive*. These passions become drives. And when they
become drives, they become wrong. That is the subtle twist.

What is wrong with eating? Why, nothing! If you don't
eat, then you won't live. But where do we cross the line between a normal satisfying of our appetites and gourmandism
and gluttony, where we live for eating, keep records of all the
restaurants that serve the finest food, study them and plan
feasts and build much of our life around them? We may actually sacrifice the relationships of life which are truly important in order that we may indulge in eating. Then it becomes
a drive, it masters us. That is what Paul is talking about
here—the drives of the body.

What is wrong with sleeping? Nothing. You may be catch-
ing up on it right now! But when you spend much of your
life sleeping and allow it to interfere with the normal development of your life, then it becomes a drive, and that is
wrong.

What is wrong with sex? Do I have to illustrate how
twisted we are in this area? There is nothing wrong with sex.
God made it. It is a perfectly proper practice of humanity.
God likes it; he designed it. But when it becomes a drive
around which we build our lives, to which we sacrifice other
values, then it becomes idolatrous. Then it is one of those
"inordinate affections," as Scripture calls them elsewhere, or

"deceitful urges" promising us much but delivering little.

Then Paul moves on to show that these drives involve not only the body—these things which concern our physical life—but also the mind, the thought life. Our thoughts can be an expression of the lusts of the flesh in this harmful sense. Here we have attitudes (such as indignation and hurt), and emotional responses (such as attraction to people). Are these wrong? No, but when they become jealousy and envy and malice and bitterness and desire for revenge they can seize us and enslave us. They can run our lives so that we build our lives around them, so that everything we do is related to some terrible envy. We want to show that we are better than someone else, or we want to get even with someone, so we spend hours and hours planning and scheming and maneuvering for revenge. That is a drive, a will of the mind.

Or take other perfectly normal things, such as reading books. Reading can be terribly wrong, if it becomes a controlling passion in our lives. Anything which controls us, for which we are ready to sacrifice normal relationships, and which begins ultimately to enslave us, is the very sort of thing he is talking about here. This is what produces the trespasses and sins which mark the death of humanity. See how subtle this is, how widespread, how deeply embedded in life, how inescapable it is. Who of us can win over this? Who can distinguish when we've passed the line? None of us is capable of it. That is why the condition of humanity is hopeless. We are all locked into death.

Now look at how it all comes out. The inevitable conclusion Paul comes to is that "we were by nature children of wrath, like the rest of mankind." We are children of wrath. We are subject to the "wrath of God." I don't know what that phrase means to you. When I once taught the book of Romans to a group of youth leaders, it became apparent to me that they had very mistaken ideas of what it means. They felt it referred to some kind of a cosmic, terrible-tempered Mr. Bang sitting up in the heavens, ready to torture fiendishly anybody who steps out of line, as though God is looking down at us as we struggle with our normal lives, shouting,

"Cut that out, or I'll zap you!" That is the usual concept of the wrath of God.

But that isn't what this phrase means. Paul analyzes it for us in Romans. The wrath of God is what we might call "the law of inevitable consequences." If we make a wrong decision it will affect us, it will hurt us, even though we intended it to be right. If I should suddenly decide to get up and walk right into a wall, I would suffer the wrath of God. I would be hurt. That wrath is designed to awaken me, to make me realize that I am violating a basic law of my own nature. If I shove my hands into my pockets and nonchalantly stroll off the top of a twenty-story building with the hope that I'll survive, I will suffer the wrath of God. It would be what you'd call "jumping to a conclusion!" There are a lot of people who are acting that way these days.

Why is it that we accept the wrath of God in physical terms without a struggle, but when it moves into the moral realm we get all upset? We say, "It isn't fair. Why shouldn't I run off with my neighbor's wife? Why shouldn't I find the happiness I deserve after years of having to live with this slob I've been married to? Why should I experience any evil results from that?" But the same kind of law applies here. Evil results will come, inevitable consequences which will destroy our humanity, tear down the beauty of human dignity within us. We will become brutalized, dehumanized, depersonalized—all of these terms are being thrown around today. That is the wrath of God.

We are subject to that wrath, Paul says, because of these great forces at work. The devil, with his clever, subtle strategies, works through the world to force us to conform to patterns which destroy, and works through the flesh, so that we move in utter naivete from a normal satisfying of human need into that excess which destroys.

Birth Defect

Furthermore, Paul says we are children of wrath *by nature.* Don't miss those two words. They mean that we are born this way. We are born into this condition, and there is nothing we can do about it! I don't know how to make that any clearer. Education, legislation, a change of environment—all these "remedies" which we propose as releases from this condition—will rearrange the pattern but will never change the basic problem. That is why humanity struggles endlessly trying to correct itself but never succeeds. Do you know of any other philosophy which can explain life in realistic terms like that, which squares with history as that does? We are born into this condition. There is no escape, no way out by ourselves. We are part of a fallen humanity.

So, Paul says, we are "like the rest of mankind." It is universal. It isn't a question of race or sex. It doesn't matter whether we are men or women, whether we are born into a civilized country or reared as savages in the jungle—the condition is still the same. There is no escape, except for the next two words, "But God . . ."

If you want to learn how to value your salvation and to praise God with a heart which is simply enraptured by what God has done, you need to understand the depths from which you have come as a Christian, the condition from which you have been released. The condition is still present in our Christian lives whenever we choose not to act upon the available resources of Jesus Christ within us. But in the non-Christian there is no hope without God, no hope. If anything should make us praise God, it is to understand fully this utterly hopeless condition in which humanity is lost, unable to help itself, struggling, miserable, wretched, unfulfilled, unsatisfied, getting worse and worse, more corrupt, and trying in all sincerity to find answers on every side. We do not disparage the efforts of men to try to find a way out, but we will never handle life properly, or understand history, until we accept this divine revelation of the condition in which we live. Then we can say at last, "But God, but God!" If you are recognizing now that you are in this condition, the answer will lie in what God has said about Jesus Christ, and in no other place, "for there is no other name under heaven given among men by which we must be saved" (Acts 4:12).

We praise you, our heavenly Father, for the fact that you are a God of such realism and truth that you dare to tell us the truth even though we don't want to hear it. You lay it before us in the simplest of terms, and we hide our eyes from it and run from it and refuse to look at it, refuse to say that it applies to us. We thank you, our Father, that you pursue us in love and work with us and bring us to experience your wrath, until we see how foolish we've been and how stupid we are, and turn at last to the only way out provided for us. Thank you for our Lord Jesus. How we rejoice in him who came and entered the race so that we might find the way out. We thank you for this and ask that it may become clearer and clearer to us, so that we will rejoice and give thanks, and live to the praise of your glory. In Jesus' name we pray, Amen.

9

BUT GOD . . .

Ephesians 2:4–6

Two little words, "But God," open the fourth verse of Ephesians 2, the chapter in which the apostle Paul sets forth the greatness of our salvation and helps us to understand what has happened to us in Jesus Christ. Nothing is more important than for us to grasp these great words:

> But God, who is rich in mercy, out of the great love with which he loved us, even when we were dead through our trespasses, made us alive together with Christ (by grace you have been saved), and raised us up with him, and made us sit with him in the heavenly places in Christ Jesus . . . (Eph. 2:4–6).

Those two words, *But God*, represent a contrast. In the opening verses of this chapter we saw what the condition of man is, as God sees him, as he actually is in life. In contrast to that gloomy picture the Apostle now says, "But God . . ."

I don't think anyone has any idea of what life would be like if God suddenly ceased his redemptive processes among us. I am sure that within hours there would be mass suicides all over the earth, because every bit of glory would be removed from life; every bit of joy, every bit of gladness, all those moments that we delight in when the family gathers around and gives us a sense of security · of warmth and joy to-

gether, all this would be gone. For these blessings come from
God's activity among men, from God at work redeeming,
reaching out, seeking to arrest the attention of men and
women and boys and girls all over the earth. If all that suddenly ceased, life would become incredibly drab and dreary.

Life teaches us that there are times when God does tem-
porarily withdraw his blessing from life and his goodness
from us, and invariably then life becomes impossible to live.
A woman was telling me about her neighbor who came across
the street one day to talk with her. He was in utter despair,
and as he sat with his head in his hands and a cup of coffee
steaming untouched in front of him, he cried out in an agony
of spirit, "God, but I'm bored!" That is the way life is for so
many—utterly miserable and meaningless.

Why is that? Well, the Apostle Paul tells us that this is
the result of the condition into which we are born. The only
thing that alleviates this misery is the mercy and the grace of
God. It would always be that way, every moment of life
would be that way, were it not for God's goodness poured out
upon us, to the just and the unjust alike, in his attempt to
reach us and arrest us. So these words come through to us
with great meaning: "But God. . . ."

Moved by Mercy

The Apostle is very careful to tell us immediately what it
is that moves God to act: "But God, who is rich in mercy,
out of the great love with which he loved us, even when we
were dead through our trespasses . . ." (Eph. 4–5b). That
was the condition in which we were found, but God was
moved to act. What moved him? He was moved first, the
Apostle says, by his mercy.

Do you understand what mercy is? And especially, what
the difference is between mercy and grace? We bandy these
terms around frequently, especially in studying the New Testament, but we often don't understand what they actually
mean, and sometimes we don't distinguish between these important words. A little boy in Sunday school was asked to tell
the difference between *kindness* and *lovingkindness*, because

Scripture uses both these words. He put it this way: "If I ask my mother for a slice of bread and butter and she gives it to me, that is kindness. But if she puts jam on it, that is loving-kindness!" That is great theological truth!

There is also a difference between mercy and grace. Mercy has to do with the withholding of a deserved penalty; grace is the supply of undeserved blessing. It is true that God's grace and his mercy both reach out to man, but each for a different reason. It is the guilt of man that draws forth the grace of God. When God looks at us and sees us as guilty— as actually having made choices and done things which were deliberately wrong when we knew them to be wrong—his compassion is called forth, expressed in grace. Even though we deserve it, he still doesn't want to leave us in our guilt. So through his grace, he reaches out to find a way to set aside the demands of law and to relieve us from the due punishment of our guilt and to set us free. It is the grace of God which has dealt with our guilt.

But it is our misery which calls forth his mercy. Parents know how this is. If your child is suffering from a severe cold—his throat is sore, his eyes are watering, his nose is running or stuffed up so he can hardly breathe; he is aching in every joint, and so miserable that all he can do is throw his arms around your neck and cry—how do you react? Your child's suffering awakens your pity, and you reach out to relieve this condition in any way you possibly can. His misery has called forth your mercy, and that is what Paul says has awakened the mercy of God—the misery of man.

Paul has already made clear that as a race we are impotent and corrupt, vulnerable to pressures to conform. We are, by nature, "children of wrath," locked into slavish obedience to impulses of the flesh. And we are controlled by Satan who keeps us on the defensive, ready to rebel and strike out at each other, because of the spirit of disobedience at work in us. The result is the heartache, the disillusionment, the boredom, and the frustration of life.

We are so aware of all this with regard to what others do to us, and so little aware of how we are doing the same thing to them. Isn't that amazing? Our image of ourselves is always so much better than what we actually are. It is so easy to forget the nasty little things we say, the sharp and caustic remarks we make, and the irritated attitudes we come to breakfast with. After a while we forget about all of these, and as we look at ourselves we see what we love to call "beautiful people," with just a slight taint here or there that a good resolution would clear up. We can't understand why life doesn't smooth out, why there is so much frustration and boredom in our experience, why we are always being so injured and hurt and cut, but God sees us realistically and he says, "Your own condition is making you miserable." And his loving mercy reaches out to us. He wants to do something to relieve the misery of man.

A Meeting of Needs

God's mercy arises from his love, and love is active. His mercy arises "out of the great love with which he loved us . . ." (Eph. 2:4). What the Apostle has in mind here is the cross, and behind it the whole story of Jesus' coming to earth. What is the sign of the love of God? How do we know that God loved us? Because "God so loved the world that he gave . . ." (John 3:16). This is always the mark of love, and we need to understand this kind of love in our relationships.

Husbands, for instance, often have a great deal of difficulty in understanding and obeying the command of Scripture, "Husbands, love your wives" (Eph. 5:25), because they don't know what love is. To most of us love is a kind of feeling, an affectionate feeling, which we do have at times towards our wives, thank God, and with which we started the whole process of marriage. But it isn't always there. Nevertheless, husbands are told to love their wives. Yet if love is nothing but this feeling, this itch around the heart that you can't scratch, this uncertain attitude which is nice to have but not always present, then it is impossible to obey that exhortation to love your wife.

But love isn't a feeling. Love is a commitment of will, a choice that you make. Love is an active moving out to meet the needs of someone else. That is why the Scriptures say, "If your enemy is hungry, give him bread to eat; and if he is thirsty, give him water to drink" (Prov. 25:21). You love somebody when you respond to his needs, and when a husband begins to meet his wife's needs—to find out who she is, where she is in life, what she wants and what she needs, and begins to work at supplying those needs—that is when he begins to love his wife. And that is how a wife can love her husband.

This is what God wants us to understand. Paul is saying, "God loved us and he did something about it. He came here." He is not a God of indifference or unconcern. He was touched with our misery and he wept and he suffered. He became the poorest of the poor; he was rejected, he felt hurt, he was frightened, he experienced all the trials which come into our lives. And when he had fully identified himself with us he went out and, in the indescribable anguish and pain of the cross, for no reason in himself, he bore our sins. Of course, Paul doesn't mention that specifically at this point; it comes in later in the epistle. But it is the background, the necessary groundwork, for what follows here. It is gathered up in the great idea of the love of God, reaching out to us. There was nothing *in us* which could help him in the least degree; we were dead in our trespasses. We have done nothing to break through this pattern of human misery.

The biblical view of life is accurate; it fits history. You can go back through history and read about all the struggles of men in the past—in the Middle Ages, at the time of our Lord, in the Golden Age of Greece, in the Persian Empire, as far back as you like—and you will find that men and women then were struggling with exactly the same problems and feeling the same hurts and the same abject miseries, and were governed by human hatred and fratricide and war just as we are. It has always been exactly the same as today.

The prophets of our day say that we have had such an explosion of knowledge, giving rise to technological possibilities men never even dreamed of before, that we ought to be able to solve the problems of life much more readily. But the truth is that we have not learned one thing about relieving human misery and hurt. Our cities today are largely great pools of human misery, stirring with hatred and strife, and ready to break out in riot and revolution at a moment's notice. That is how much all the knowledge humans have gathered through the centuries has meant in actually solving this human condition.

When we were dead, when we were absolutely hopeless, then God did something. This is what the Apostle wants us to see. God took action. God broke through. And what he accomplished did break the spell of evil, and began to set us free, when we believed in Jesus Christ.

Now the Apostle moves to help us understand what happened when we believed. What did God do to break this pattern, and how does it work? I don't hesitate to say that if we fail to understand this clearly we will never be able to enter into the riches that are ours in Jesus Christ. We will always be groveling around, trying to live a good Christian life, struggling and discovering a few helpful things here and there, but watching others go on into freedom and liberty and joyfulness and beauty of character, while we ourselves never seem able to discover the secret. We must understand thoroughly what has happened to us.

Three things are brought out by the Apostle Paul: First, he says, God "made us alive together with Christ" (Eph. 2:5) and in parentheses he reminds us "(by grace you have been saved)." It is the grace of God, and not the activity of man that saves us. There is not one thing which man can add to this work of redeeming broken human lives. Second; we have been "raised up with him" (v. 6), and third, "made to sit with him in the heavenly places in Christ Jesus" (v. 6). Those are not merely theological phrases. They represent realities which have already happened and which we need desperately to understand.

Enlivened with Christ

We will take only the first of these in this chapter. Examine with me the phrase, "made us alive together with Christ."

In the Greek language, "made us alive together with" is all one word; he *enlivened* us, with Christ. There you have the central secret of the Christian life. We were made alive in Christ. That happened when we believed in Jesus.

Many people don't experience very much when they become Christians. It is usually a quiet time, perhaps accompanied by a slight sense of peace. With some there is a sense of joy, but it is usually not very dramatic. I have had the joy of leading many to Christ, and almost always it is very, very quiet. And yet, a tremendous thing has happened! It is the difference between death and life!

What occurs in the inner life of man when he believes in Jesus Christ is as dramatic, as complete a contrast with the old life as between a cold, stiff corpse and a warm, breathing, living man. We are no longer dead when we believe. We are alive in Jesus Christ. A life has been imparted to us.

There are a great many similes in Scripture to help us understand truth. One of them is the process of birth. Becoming a Christian is likened to being born. But where does birth start? We know that it doesn't start with the actual entrance of the baby into the world. It starts with conception. Conception takes place in an act of love when the ovum and the sperm are joined together. But the mother doesn't know anything about it—she doesn't feel that. Yet a remarkable thing has occurred within her body, something which she doesn't sense but which, nevertheless, will change her life and perhaps the history of the entire world, as many babies have changed the history of the world when they grew up. That is exactly the kind of thing Paul brings to our attention here. When we are born again in Jesus Christ we receive life from him. We're made one spirit with him. We are no longer dead, no longer unresponsive to God. We are made alive in Jesus Christ.

Signs of New Life

It is helpful, in trying to understand this, to realize that something happens to our attitudes. We simply are not the same person from that time on, and it begins to show almost immediately. I have learned, for instance, to start looking for a certain sign within moments after a person becomes a Christian. His self-centeredness ends, momentarily at least, and he begins to think of someone else. I have seen this happen so many times at the moment someone has come to Christ and has had a minute or two to think of what has happened to him. So often he will say, "Oh, I wish you would tell this to my brother," or, "I wish you'd pray about my parents." Immediately his thoughts turn away from his own experience to someone else with whom he wants to share it. That is a sign of passing from death into life.

There is also an immediate change in our attitude toward God. Have you noticed that most non-Christians are afraid of God? They don't want to come around church because they see people enjoying the presence of God there, and it makes them feel uneasy. That is perfectly all right; they shouldn't be expected to come to church in order to find God. God reaches out to them where they are, through his people. But they are afraid of God. And this is why they are afraid of death, why non-Christians don't like even the thought of death. At a funeral they are restless and uneasy and nervous, hoping to get the whole thing over as quickly as possible so they can get back to the familiar surroundings of a bar or their home—wherever they can escape the thought of death. Why don't they like death? Because they know that it introduces them to the presence of God, and they don't want God. They are running and hiding from him.

But when they become Christians that changes immediately; God is now their Father. They have a sense of belonging. And now the one person they want above all others is God, and they cry as did the Psalmist, "As a hart longs for flowing streams, so longs my soul for thee, O God" (Ps. 42:1). "The Lord is my Shepherd, I shall not want" (Ps. 23:1). Immediately there is a hunger for God. That is a mark of passing from death to life. They are beginning to live as God intends men to live.

But the greatest thing of all, of course, the most important truth in all of Christianity, is stated right here: "We are made alive together *with Christ.*" Notice that Paul says "with Christ" three times: "We are made alive together *with Christ.*" "We are raised up *with him.*" "We are made to sit *with him.*" The greatest fact of all is that we are joined to Jesus Christ. He has come to live in us. And more than just coming to live in us he has joined himself to us, and we are one person with him. That is the most important fact upon which to build the rest of Christian faith and experience—this great, tremendous statement that we are made alive with Jesus Christ, joined with him.

Do you remember how the Lord himself taught that? He said, "I am the vine, you are the branches" (John 15:5). Can you tell where the branch ends and the vine starts? No. They are one plant, sharing one life together. So from here on our identity is no longer "in Adam" but it is "in Christ." We are no longer just ordinary human beings. We are new creations, begun again, linked with the life of Jesus Christ. That is our identity from the moment we believe.

Later in this letter, Paul likens the church to a body of which Christ is the head. Have you examined your body lately? Have you noticed, for instance, that your fingers don't come off if you twist them a halfturn and pull? They are tied to the body. They share the life of the body. They are not attached by any mechanical process. They are an organic part of it. In just such an intimate way, we are united to Jesus Christ; he is our life.

So never think of yourself in any other way, because the whole work of the enemy is to get you to disbelieve that, and to go back to thinking you are just an ordinary individual, struggling on through life, needing to mobilize all your human resources to try to get ahead of the other fellow. But any time you believe that, you go right back to acting as you once did, back to the misery, back to the heartaches. You can escape that only when you return to this central truth—we are alive in Jesus Christ!

There is one final thing to notice here; these verbs are all in the past tense. God *has made* us alive together with Christ; he *has raised* us up, and *has made* us sit with him. All this has already occurred when you believe in Jesus Christ. You don't have to work toward it. It is not something which great saints achieve after years of effort. It is something which is already true, and every Christian has this experience. We were made alive in Jesus Christ. We are not the same. We cannot be the same again, anymore. We cannot go back to living the way we once did. Even if we try we won't be able to. A new humanity has begun.

Never let yourself forget the great fact that you are changed, that you are a new creation, that you have begun a new relationship. There is no way you can erase it, and no way you can lose it. You are made alive together with Christ.

Heavenly Father, we give thanks to you for this great truth. We, Lord, ask you to make plain what this means—that this is who we are, and that we will never be able to handle life aright until we first know who we are. Help us to remember this, and impress it on our hearts and minds again and again, that we have been made alive in Jesus Christ, called out of darkness into light, delivered from the power of Satan into the kingdom of God, and made new creatures in Jesus Christ. We thank you in his name, Amen.

10

ALIVE TO LIVE

Ephesians 2:4–6

Any psychologist will tell you that the basic solution to any mental problem is one of identity. The basic crisis of our day is an identity crisis. If we are going to solve the problems of our lives, we must know who we are. So the Apostle Paul is very careful to set forth in the second chapter of Ephesians exactly who we are in Christ. The worst struggles most of us have with our Christian faith come when we try to work out our problems without this foundation, without realizing who we are in Jesus Christ.

We have already seen the depths of depravity and darkness from which the Lord Jesus lifts us. Then we saw, beginning in verse 4, the fantastic change which was introduced by the words "But God." And that is where we want to start again:

> But God, who is rich in mercy, out of the great love with which he loved us, even when we were dead through our trespasses, made us alive together with Christ (by grace you have been saved), and raised us up with him, and made us sit with him in the heavenly places in Christ Jesus, that in the coming ages he might show the immeasurable riches of his grace in kindness toward us in Christ Jesus (Eph. 2:4–7).

You will notice that when he is talking about who we are as Christians, the Apostle draws an exact parallel to the experience of the Lord himself. He identifies us with what Jesus has gone through. We died with him (we learn this also in Romans 6). Then we are made alive together with him. Finally, we are raised up with him and made to sit with him in the heavenly places in Christ Jesus. These phrases are designed to teach us something about ourselves and who we are as Christians. It is necessary, therefore, that we understand what these phrases actually mean in terms of our experience.

We have already considered what it means to be alive in Christ, to be "made alive together with him." First of all, remember, it means that we are no longer dead, that the condition into which we were born has been changed. We are no longer alienated and afraid of God. When a person comes to Jesus Christ, he is no longer afraid of death, because he is no longer afraid to confront God. God is not seen any longer as his enemy, as a terrible judge, an avenger. Rather, he is seen as a friend, as a father, with a father's love, a father's arms, and a father's heart.

Further, we saw that being made alive in Christ means we are joined to him. Somehow we have been identified with him. His life has become our life, and our new identity *is Christ*. He is our life. "But he who is united to the Lord becomes one spirit with him" (1 Cor. 6:17). So from then on we must never think of ourselves as what we once were in Adam. We are *in Christ*. We belong to him. He has welded himself to us so that an unbreakable union has been established, and we are his and he is ours. According to his own words, it is "You in me and I in you," and nothing can break this relationship.

This means, of course, that we are changed to the very depths of our being. Something happened to us when we came to Jesus Christ which alters everything we are from that moment on. We are absolutely different. We are changed at the very root-level of our life, fundamentally and foundationally, so that we have a different outlook, different attitudes, and a different approach to situations. Rather startling and dramatic changes sometimes occur.

Not long ago we received a package in the mail at the church. We opened it, and to our amazement and bewilderment we found that it was a package of birth control pills. Who would send birth control pills to a church? We opened the card that came with the package and read:

Dear PBC: The prescription for these pills dates to October. They are still good. Use them if you like. I no longer need them, as I am reformed, though not married. Praise the Lord! He is holding me up.

It was signed "The little toe of the Body." We didn't ask for that testimony and didn't know it was coming. But it was a sign of a basic change in a person who was made alive in Jesus Christ.

Now what happens in our experience as this new life begins to work itself out? The Apostle adds two other factors which are fundamental to this new relationship we have in Christ. We are "raised up with him," and "made to sit with him in the heavenly places." Again, this follows the parallel of what happened to Jesus. What happened to him is what happens to us. He died. When they took his body down from the cross it gave every evidence, it had all the marks, of death. Rigor mortis had set in. It was cold and stiff. A painting I once saw entitled "The Descent from the Cross" showed in stark and grisly detail the terrible fact of the death of Jesus. The mouth was open, the teeth were protruding, the eyes were glazed. It was obvious that this was a dead body. And that dead body was laid in the tomb. The grim reality of that death cast a pall of gloom over the apostles, dashing their hopes and putting an end to all their dreams. The Lord was dead.

But on the third morning God the Father infused into that dead body new life, and Jesus was made alive. "And that," says the Apostle Paul, "is exactly what happened to us when we were made alive in Christ. Into the death of our fallen humanity there came a new life, a new Spirit."

New Approach to Old Circumstances

Of course, the resurrected Jesus did not continue to live in the tomb. This is the next point the Apostle makes. He didn't remain there holding counseling sessions with people who came to visit him. No, he was raised up and put back into business. He was thrust back into the experiences of men, but on an entirely different basis. This is what the Apostle says happened to us when we were made alive in Christ, so it is important for us to see this. We are called to go back, as Jesus did, into the same circumstances, into the same situation, but to reckon on a new power, to demonstrate the power of resurrection life.

Resurrection power means that the Christian is able to do what he could never do by himself. He is able to act in a way which is impossible to those who are without Jesus Christ. For example, he is able to love the unlovable, to endure the unendurable, to achieve the unachievable, and to forgive the unforgivable. Many a husband has told me that he had reached such a state of estrangement in his marriage that he literally hated his wife, couldn't stand the sight of her, couldn't abide her presence. But after he became a Christian a new relationship was born. He was able, despite struggles, to begin to look at his wife in a new way and actually begin to love her. Many wives have said the same thing about their husbands.

Young people have told me how they hated their parents, had come to the place where they couldn't stand them a moment longer; everything their parents did turned them off. They regarded them as nothing but rivals and obstacles to everything they wanted to do. But after coming to Christ, they found it possible to come to a new sense of appreciation and understanding, and love for their parents began to bloom again. With pity and compassion they saw them as people like themselves, struggling with difficult problems they too were unable to handle. All this was possible because they were raised up and sent back into life again, to handle the same problems, but with a different outlook.

Some have learned to endure the unendurable. I know of a woman who for thirteen years has been unable to move about normally. She has gone through terrible struggles with depression, discouragement, and defeat, but the Lord has sustained her and kept her through this time. Gradually she has been able to come to a place of rest and contentment. And, although she has been close to it, she has never taken the way out which her mind suggested to her from time to time—a bottle of pills, or some other method of suicide. She has been able to endure because of the power released in her by a risen Lord.

There are some who have been able to achieve the unachievable. The Job Therapy program in California prisons is a good illustration of this. When the program's promoters first went into certain prisons, the wardens were very suspicious and didn't feel it would ever accomplish anything. But as the promoters explained that it would put prisoners in touch with Christian families who would visit them, make friends with them, and be available to meet whatever needs they might have when they got out, the wardens were willing to give it a chance. Recently some of these wardens have testified that the program has begun to change the atmosphere in their prisons. Many of the prisons in this country are seething with revolt and discontent, ready to erupt in violence at any moment. But a new hope has begun to spread. "Salt" has been introduced, and change for the better is beginning. This is the power of a resurrected Lord. This is what "raised up with him" means—to come to life again with a new approach and a new power.

It also means the ability to forgive the unforgivable. When singer-composer John Fischer was in Southern California a few years ago he sang in the chapel of a certain Christian college. Afterward, one of the professors of the school wrote a scurrilous letter to the school paper in which he bitterly attacked John and his music, sarcastically labeling it "musical garbage." When John read the paper he was upset and angry. He was tempted to write this man off as obviously having no musical judgment whatsoever, and to feel resentful toward him for taking such a position.

But then the Lord began to speak to him, and said, "It isn't right for you to feel that way. This man shared how he felt in all honesty. You may not agree with him, but nevertheless you have no right to be resentful toward him." So

John determined to take a Christian approach. The next time he was in the area he looked this man up and took him out to dinner. They sat down together in a rather strained atmosphere, at first, as you can imagine. The man didn't know what John wanted. But John asked him something about his background, and it wasn't very long before they found a mutual interest and began to explore it. This led to other topics. The upshot was that after two hours they felt as close to one another as though they were brothers. They enjoyed a wonderful time together, and the subject of the letter never once came up. They simply appreciated each other. Later on this man heard that John was giving a concert some distance away. To John's surprise he showed up and listened to him play. He came to him afterward and told him how much his son appreciated John's music! The healing had started.

Designed to Dissolve

That is the power of resurrection life. It is designed to confound the calculations of men, to transform the demoralized, and not so much to solve as to dissolve the problems of life. Resurrection power works differently. It means that we come at life with a different attitude which often baffles and bewilders people. They can't figure it out, but they recognize that it does wonderful things. That is what it means to be raised up together with him.

The third factor involved in our basic relationship with Christ—part of our true identity—is that not only have we been made alive and raised up with him, but we have been made to sit with him in the heavenly places in Christ Jesus. What does that mean? In several places in Scripture Christ is said to have been raised up and made to sit at the right hand of God. In Hebrews 1:13, the writer says that no angel can ever compare with Christ because, as he puts it:

> But to what angel has he ever said,
> "Sit at my right hand,
> till I make thy enemies
> a stool for thy feet"?

In the tenth chapter of the same book there is another reference:

> But when Christ had offered for all time a single sacrifice for sins, he sat down at the right hand of God, then to wait until his enemies should be made a stool for his feet (Heb. 10: 12–13).

Why is Christ said to have "sat down" when he came to the right hand of the Father after his ascension? It surely does not mean that he sits up there somewhere in a chair, waiting. It is obviously a picture, a symbol of something. Well, what does sitting symbolize? It symbolizes cessation of effort. Sitting means the end of work and of strain. It is a beautiful picture of what the Scriptures call "rest." We often sing Jean Pigott's hymn:

> Jesus, I am resting, resting
> In the joy of what Thou art;
> I am finding out the greatness
> Of Thy loving heart.

It means dependence upon the work of another. If you were working away digging a hole, sweating and straining and tired and exhausted, and I came along and said, "Look, why don't you rest? I'll take over," what would you expect me to do? Would you expect me to exhort you to try harder, get a sharper shovel, dig deeper? No. If I meant what I said, I would want you to get out of the hole and let me take the shovel while you sat down and relaxed. I would do the work. And this is the picture drawn for us of what a Christian is to do. He is to live as seated with Christ in the heavenlies. The heavenlies, of course, is not some far distant spot in space where heaven is. It is the invisible realm of reality—the inner life, the place where we feel tension and pressure and anxiety and hostility. We are to rest there. Having done what Jesus asks us to do, we are to sit down and rest, relax, and let him bear the pressure and the problems.

Puzzling Efficiency

It is amazing how difficult this is for Christians to grasp. I know a very successful businessman who, although he is a Christian, has never been taught very much in this realm. He has naturally applied much of his business practice to his Christian life. And much of it can be applied. He has learned the necessity of planning goals and of moving toward them with smooth organization, thus bringing about the desired results. But he confessed himself to be utterly baffled by the way we operate at PBC. He said he was fascinated but mystified, because it looks as if we are so loose, and yet it is amazing how everything works out. He said, "I have been counting the mistakes you made. And every one of those mistakes was the turning point that produced the good results which followed. I can't understand it!" He is learning the great fact that it isn't up to us to maneuver and manipulate to obtain the proper results. We are dealing with a God who has announced that he has ways of working which go beyond what we are able to do. He has told us that he is able to do exceeding abundantly above all that we can ask or think. So it is no good trying to sit down and reason out what he is going to do, because you can't ask or think what it is. He has announced through Isaiah:

> For my thoughts are not your thoughts,
>   neither are your ways my ways, says the Lord.
> For as the heavens are higher than the earth,
>   so are my ways higher than your ways
>   and my thoughts than your thoughts (Isa. 55:8–9).

We have to cry out with Paul:

> O the depths of the riches and wisdom and knowledge of God! How unsearchable are his judgments and how inscrutable his ways! (Rom. 11:33).

Do you see how resting in Jesus can turn life into an adventure? You never know how any situation will turn out. A

creative God, beginning to work in the most ordinary circumstances, can suddenly make them break wide open, and you
have something on your hands which staggers you, which you
never dreamed could happen, and which even alarms you, so
vast are its possibilities. This is the kind of God we have. So
having done what is expected or required, we are to sit, expecting him to work, and resting without anxiety, free from
struggling, straining, and striving.

Hope Does Not Disappoint Us

There is one other factor involved in rest. The passage in
Hebrews tells us that when Jesus sat down at the right hand of
the Father, he was waiting "till his enemies were made his
footstool." He was waiting until God the Father, working
with the principles involved in the cross and the resurrection,
produces harmony and peace once again in creation. Then
every force opposed to the authority of Jesus Christ will be
subdued, and every knee shall bow and confess that Jesus is
Lord, to the glory of God the Father. In other words, he is
waiting for an absolutely certain result, but it won't come
quickly.

That is our problem. What this figure of sitting involves is
the expectation of a certain result, yet it is one we must wait
for with patience. Here is where we struggle. Perhaps the
most difficult struggle in the Christian life is with the slow-
ness of God. Have you found out how incredibly slow he is
at times? Do you get as impatient with him as I do? There
are times when it is as clear as daylight to me how he ought
to act. I can outline the steps for him—and I do! I tell him
just what to do, and it would all work out if he would just
take those steps. But he utterly ignores me and goes on doing
nothing until I want to rise up and say, "Look, you've got to
get off your throne and do something!" I struggle at this
point. But God goes on waiting and then, suddenly, before I
know it, what I had hoped—and more than I'd ever hoped—
has happened. Sometimes I don't even know how it came
about.

Some things I am still waiting for, but this is the point: The Lord tells us that his work is like a farmer going out to sow his seed. The farmer scatters his seed, and then Jesus says he goes home and goes to bed. He rests; he relaxes and lets the seed grow, because that is the nature of seed. It must go through a certain process involving time; no seed drops into the ground and springs up suddenly. You must allow it to decay, to deteriorate, to fall apart, and then out of that comes a new life—it will grow slowly and steadily into the air until finally the whole plant is before you. God announces that this is his way of working. He urges us to understand that the result is certain, and on that we can rest patiently, knowing that he is working out his purposes. We are seated with him in the heavenly places.

I would like to make three observations concerning the relationship Paul has described for us here. First, this is true Christianity. Anything else is a fraud. Any effort to try to be religious or Christian which doesn't stem from this three-fold relationship of being made alive in Christ, raised with new power, and put back into life to rest in his activity and the certainty of his accomplishing his work, is a counterfeit of the Christian life. It is "godliness" without God, "Christianity" without Christ, "spirituality" without the Spirit. And it can never accomplish anything except ultimately to turn people away. What Paul has outlined for us here, and this alone, is true Christianity.

Second, as I mentioned earlier, these three great facts are already true of every regenerated Christian. They may not be in your experience yet, however, because of two factors: first, ignorance. You might not have begun to experience this because you were unaware of this relationship. Most of us don't have much understanding of it. We don't approach our problems this way, so we need to know more about it. Second, it may not be true in your experience because you love the pleasures the flesh can give you more than those of the Spirit. We all love the twisted, perverted pleasure of acting in the flesh, in the old way—the self-effort, the self-pleasing, self-indulgent life. Christians choose that way at times, but when we do, we ought to remember that we have not lost this three-fold relationship. We can always return to it because it is not temporary; it is a permanent fixture in our lives. When we acknowledge the evil, the flesh to which we have submitted, we can return to this relationship.

The third observation is this: This relationship becomes observable and actual by faith, that is, by actually living and acting on this basis, by trusting these facts as true and acting accordingly. That is faith. This is no mere armchair theology. There are no easy choices here. We are called on to obey these facts when the flesh within us is screaming for revenge, or when the heart faints with discouragement and despair and we are ready to give up, or when the temptation to be lustful or bitter or sarcastic sweeps over us in waves. We may only claim this relationship for moments at a time and must renew it again and again until at last we enter into some degree of calm and quiet. It is a battle.

But it is always possible to win. Each time temptation occurs, we are to remind ourselves, "I am alive in Christ. I am not the same person. I am no longer what I once was. I may not be what I ought to be, but thank God I am not what I was! I am alive in Christ and I am raised with him. I have a new power at my disposal—the power of his life in me. Therefore I can rest. I can step out and say and do the ordinary thing, and expect him to accomplish the results. I can relax. I don't have to strain. I can leave the problem of solving the difficult situations in his hands, and I will wait for the ultimate and certain result."

To do this is to learn to let God be God. This is the way God works. This is the way the life of God is released in the human situation. What a tremendous basis for living! This is our identity from now on. It is who we are. Start every day on this basis, and meet every situation on this basis.

I have been crucified with Christ; it is no longer I who live, but Christ who lives in me; and the life I now live in the flesh I live by faith in the Son of God, who loved me and gave himself for me (Gal. 2:20).

Our heavenly Father, we thank you for this marvelous picture which is true of us. You see life as it really is, so this is true of us. We pray that you will enable us to grasp it, to understand it, and to begin to handle the problems now before us on this basis. In Christ's name, Amen.

11

ON DISPLAY

Ephesians 2:7–10

We have tried to grasp what it means and how essential it is to approach life on the basis of our identity with Christ. Now, beginning with verse 7, we look beyond our present experience to the future that lies ahead of us. The Apostle says that God has . . . made us alive with Christ, raised us up, and seated us with him, so that

> . . . in the coming ages he might show the immeasurable riches of his grace in kindness toward us in Christ Jesus. For by grace you have been saved through faith; and this is not your own doing, it is the gift of God—not because of works, lest any man should boast. For we are his workmanship, created in Christ Jesus for good works, which God prepared beforehand, that we should walk in them (Eph. 2:7–10).

Immediately Paul explores the purpose of God in redeeming mankind. Why does he come into our lives? Why does he change the fundamental basis of our experience? The answer is that in the coming ages he plans to display the immeasurable riches of his grace through his kindness to us in Christ Jesus. In other words, God's purpose in doing all this is that he might have a display case in which his grace—the glory of his character and being—will become fully evident.

Some time ago my family and I went to the De Young

Museum in San Francisco's Golden Gate Park. Along with many other citizens of this area, we visited the Norman Rockwell exhibit of paintings. I have long enjoyed his paintings, especially when they appeared on the cover of the *Saturday Evening Post* for so many years. Many of the originals of those *Post* covers were in this exhibit, so that a rich slice of Americana was spread before us. Each of those paintings is a display of the skill of the artist and of his ability to capture some passing mood, some look, some situation which would evoke either humor or a sense of nostalgia. I stood before one picture and laughed out loud it was so funny, and another almost brought me to tears.

This is exactly the thought the Apostle has in mind here. God is going to put us on display. Each one of us will be a vivid demonstration of the grace and perfection of God's character. The glory of his Person will be visible in us throughout the coming ages; especially will it be manifested, says Paul, by his kindness toward us.

Natural Blessings

If you want to know more about the kindness of God, you need only take a concordance and trace this word through the Scriptures. You will find, for instance, that it is used to refer to the goodness of God to us as reflected in natural life. The fourteenth chapter of the book of Acts records that the Apostle Paul and his companion Barnabas preached to the people in Lystra. Among other things, Paul said:

In past generations he allowed all the nations to walk in their own ways; yet he did not leave himself without witness, for he did good and gave you from heaven rains and fruitful seasons, satisfying your hearts with food and gladness (Acts 14:16–17).

I hope every one of you stops frequently to give thanks to God for his goodness in nature, for the abundance of supply given to us in this richly favored land of ours. It is right that we should, because this is a mark of God's kindness toward us. Paul argues further along this line in the second chapter of

Romans. He says to the pagan world, "Do you presume upon the riches of his [God's] kindness and forbearance and patience? Do you not know that God's kindness is meant to lead you to repentance?" (Rom. 2:4). That is, it is designed to make you think about the God who loves you enough to supply your needs and to fill your life with richness of food and shelter and clothing and all the other things God has given you.

But this kindness is not confined to natural blessings; it is also redemptive. This same word appears in the letter to Titus, where Paul says, "When the goodness and loving kindness of God our Savior appeared, he saved us, . . . by the washing of regeneration and renewal in the Holy Spirit" (Titus 3:4–5). All this is meant to remind us of the way God works in our lives. Do you ever stop to think about these things? Do you wake up every morning and give thanks for the food, the clothing, the shelter, and all the other things God has given to you?

How Long Is an Age?

According to the Apostle, God has just begun to give. He has not yet poured his kindness out upon us to its full degree. His program, Paul says, is to manifest in abundance the riches of his grace in his kindness toward us through the coming *ages*. If you read a passage like that without stopping to think a bit, you've missed the full impact of this truth. How long is an age? Well, according to the Scriptures, there have been only two ages in the history of man, so far. One was the age from Adam to the Flood of Noah. The other is the age from the Flood to the present day. It will end at the coming again of the Lord Jesus, when another age will begin. But according to this passage in Ephesians, God has in mind many ages yet to come. You'll notice that the word is in the plural: "in the coming ages." How long will that be? Well, who can say what is in the heart and mind of God? But what the passage does declare to us is that God has in mind possibilities in the future far more extensive than anything we have yet dreamed.

What we have already tasted is only a mere "trickle" of his grace; yet it is so rich and abundant that it blows the fuses of our understanding when we begin to realize what we already have. Paul says that grace will increase more and more so that in the coming ages God might demonstrate his kindness. I hope this helps you to grasp something of the majestic greatness of the God who has already so richly blessed our lives. If you have experienced anything of what it means to be made alive in Christ, to be raised up with him, you know how rich your life has become already. But that is just the beginning. It is to continue in the coming ages.

We have only the briefest hints in Scripture as to the full intent of God for us, the amazing possibilities ahead in the realm of physical experience. It is clear that God's kindness will unfold increasingly in a natural, physical sense, as well as in a spiritual sense. There are tantalizing references to the new heavens and new earth, to a resurrected body, equipped to meet all the demands of the human spirit. In these references we are given but a glimpse of what lies ahead for those who are in Jesus Christ.

I have long been interested in astronomy and am always fascinated to read about the enormous telescopes such as those on Mt. Hamilton and on Mt. Palomar in California. They are looking in the front window of the Father's house! When I look into the heavens and think of the vast reaches of the universe, the innumerable galaxies whirling out there in space, it is inconceivable to me that God would create this far-flung universe without intending to develop it further. The Scriptures certainly suggest that in the coming ages we who have found Jesus Christ and are learning how to operate according to the ways God himself is teaching us—to walk and live by faith in dependence upon his life—shall be given fantastic opportunities to help develop God's universe. We may conquer worlds perhaps already occupied, who knows? (I believe the Scriptures indicate that there are other beings in the universe.) Paul does not detail these possibilities for us here, but he hints that in these coming ages, age upon age, there will be tremendous work to do, and tremendous equipment with which to do it. God will constantly be increasing the display in us of his kindness. I must leave it there, but I suggest that this concept merits considerable study.

One thing this passage does make clear—it reveals our present puny experience in its proper perspective. If your thinking is bounded only by the womb and the tomb, what a brief span of life you are engaged in, what piddling possibilities you are concerned with! God has far greater prospects ahead, and the believer is invited to lift his eyes from this present experience. Our present life might not always be what we'd like it to be. In fact, we are guaranteed that it won't be. But it is merely the beginning, the start toward immeasurable possibilities which lie beyond. Robert Browning's poem "Rabbi Ben Ezra" takes on new meaning in light of a passage like this.

> Grow old along with me!
> The best is yet to be,
> The last of life, for which the first was made.

We are learning now, in this age, in order that we might be prepared to display the greatness of God's glory in the coming ages.

Next Paul brings the basis for all this before us again. He never lets us forget why and how this can be:

For by grace you have been saved through faith; and this is not your own doing, it is the gift of God—not because of works, lest any man should boast (Eph. 2:8–9).

Grace is what makes it all possible. Just think of it! It has already been done. Notice the tense of the verb: "You have been saved." This refers back to the three-fold relationship Paul has already set forth. We have been made alive in Christ. We have been given a new identity. We are no longer what we once were. We are no longer associated with Adam; we are in Christ, and Christ is our life. We face every day, every moment, no longer a child of Adam, born to a fallen condition, but as a son of the living God.

Truth That Delivers

I cannot stress enough how important that is to remember! It will make all the difference in the world as to whether you approach life feeling inadequate, guilty, rejected, and lonely, or whether you are filled with confidence, certainty, acceptance, love, and warmth. It will make all the difference in the world as to how you begin each day, and how you think of yourself before God. The truth is, as psychologists tell us, that if you do not see yourself as a worthwhile person, accepted before God and of great importance to him, then you can not see anyone else that way. You will begin to demand performance of others in order to accept them. You will not be able to forgive others. You will be caught up in a web of perfectionism in which you are constantly feeling guilty yourself, because you don't live up to your own ideals.

What delivers you from that are the tremendous facts set forth here. We have a new identity in Jesus Christ, a new power. We are raised up together with him. His power is available to us in the ordinary circumstances of our lives. God himself is present, and is releasing through us—in ways we cannot feel but nevertheless are true—his life, a touch of heaven upon our earthly condition. And we can enter into a new attitude. We are made to sit together with him in heavenly places in Christ. We are to rest in him, to relax and let him carry the load, and to be freed from strain, anxiety, and fear of what the outcome will be. It is his responsibility to work out our problems.

If you are thinking of these facts as mere theological doctrines, how far astray you have gone! These are realities which make a difference as to how life is lived, what your days are like, and what your tomorrows will be. The basis, Paul reminds us, is all there; it has all been accomplished. The whole of your future development, not only in this age but in the ages to come, rests upon a foundation which has already been laid. God is not going to add another thing to it. He does not need to do another thing for you beyond what he has already done. He will simply help you to work out your life, day by day, on the basis of what has already happened.

This saves you from the silly need to run after every new theological fad that comes along, every new book that comes out, every new tape, every new program, thinking you need to have some vast new experience which will change your whole life. No, you need only grasp and understand more fully, and then put into practice the riches of God's grace already provided for you in Jesus Christ. All of the advance of your spiritual life rests upon that.

Paul stresses the fact that you had nothing to do with all this. It is God's activity. We didn't originate it; it is not our own doing. We couldn't have come up with this redemptive program by which, in a very real sense, we have died. Man never plans to die; he plans to live. Death is what he fears most. Yet God has worked out a way by which our old life can end, can die, can be put aside. We never could have thought that up. But God did, so it is not of our doing. And it is not of our deserving; we have no merit here. It is not of works, Paul says; we cannot earn it. It is all of grace, given to us, day by day, from the hand of God.

No Grounds for Boasting

God has given us this grace freely, in order that we may never boast. Do you know what boasting is? It is deceiving yourself, pretending you are something you are not. When you boast you are saying, "I'm my own creator, my own god. I have in myself what it takes to handle life. Nobody contributes to me. I am sufficient in myself." That is what we really mean when we boast. But this is a lie, because we are not self-sufficient. Each one of us is a dependent creature. We cannot live a moment without somebody else's love, without somebody else's acceptance, somebody else's understanding. Life turns dull and barren without the relationships we have with others. When we forget we are dependent creatures, lie to ourselves about it, and boast about what we have done and how much we have been able to accomplish, we are only deceiving ourselves.

God never allows such self-deception to stand. God is an utter realist. He deals with life exactly as it is. So he says that all you and I can do is to receive his grace, simply take it, moment by moment accepting relationship with him. All we can do is to utilize the power he makes available to us, and rest in the fantastic fact that he will solve all the riddles which arise, so as to accomplish the ends he has promised.

Boasting in your faith would be like boasting in the fact that you reached out to take a check from somebody. Suppose you have a tremendous debt but someone offers to pay it for you, and writes out a check for you for $500,000. And you reach out and take it from him. How absurd it would be if you then went around saying to everybody, "Isn't it wonderful that I had what it took to reach out and grab that check?" They might say to you, "Wasn't it marvelous that he paid that debt for you?" If you said, "Oh, he didn't do anything much: *I* took the check"—how silly that would be! It is the resources of God which make all this possible. It is the greatness of God which supplies this richness of grace to our lives.

So the apostle goes on now to show us its ultimate manifestation:

> For we are his workmanship, created in Christ Jesus for good works, which God prepared beforehand, that we should walk in them (Eph. 2:10).

Notice how careful he is to put "works" in the right place. You don't obtain anything from God by working for it. You never deserve anything but judgment at his hand. If he gave us what we deserve, we would all end up in hell. No. We receive his grace, his mercy, his love, which results in good works. That is the point. We are designed to produce good works.

The word translated *workmanship* is the word from which *poem* is derived. We are his poem. Or, if you like, it might be better rendered, "We are his masterpiece." God is working out in our lives a tremendous exhibition and demonstration of his wisdom, his power, his love, his life, his character, his peace, and his joy. He is teaching us, training us, bringing us along, applying the paint in exactly the right places, producing a marvelous masterpiece to be put on display. This is to result in good works: kindness, love, mercy, compassion, helping one another, meeting one another's needs.

Step into Good Works

Paul says that God has prepared these works beforehand. I have frequently experienced the truth of this. One illustration of it occurred in Albuquerque where I had gone with one of our interns. We decided, as the plane was coming in for landing, to have prayer together there on the plane. I hadn't talked to Brian about this passage at all, but I was struck by the way he prayed. He said, "Father, thank you for the good works already prepared for us in Albuquerque, for the fact that they are waiting for us to step into them and experience them." This is exactly what this passage means. God has already prepared some good works for you to do. As you walk in the Spirit, he will lead you to them. When you enter into them they will always be works of blessing, of help, of strengthening toward others.

Sure enough, after we got to Albuquerque these good works began to unfold. There was a missionary there from the Amazon region of South America who was discouraged and terribly upset, ready to quit the ministry. During the time we had there he came alive and began to see again what God could do. He came to us with a light on his face and said, "I'm going back to my field completely revolutionized in my approach. Now I've learned how God operates." A girl came to see me because she was in conflict with her parents. She did not know how to handle it. We looked together at the Scriptures and they began to unfold for her. She went home and talked with her parents, and the next day she said, "Oh, things are so much better now because I could approach them this new way!" One morning Brian had a Bible study with the wealthy businessman at whose home we were staying. It was a joy to hear him teach this man. Prominent businessman that he was, he sat as a little child at Brian's feet and learned how to study the Bible. His life was enriched by that experience. A young pastor was facing dissension in his church. He wanted counsel on how to handle it. God enabled the Scriptures to speak to that situation and give him wisdom and guidance for it. All these good works had been prepared beforehand. All we did was step into them.

Do you have any idea how many good works God has prepared for you? They are waiting for you to enter into, as you walk in faith and trust and dependence upon Christ. They are entered by faith, by trust in the God who has raised us up with Christ and made us to sit together with him. The situations are there, ready and waiting for you to step into. This is what God has called you to, and as you do, you become a vivid display of the greatness and the glory of God.

Let these thoughts rest in your heart and mind. Give thanks to God for what he has done in Jesus Christ, and for the fact that this opens to us fantastic possibilities which stretch from this moment on beyond death into the coming ages, age following upon age, incredible numbers of possibilities for the manifestation of the greatness of our God.

12

STRANGERS IN DARKNESS

Ephesians 2:11–13

If we ever really grasp what it means to be a Christian, we will never again be envious of anyone who is not a Christian. We will never wish we were back in the world, nor will we in any way be drawn toward its outlook or its pattern of life.

One way we learn to appreciate what has happened to us, of course, is by looking back to what we were and really beginning to understand what God called us out of in Christ. The opening words of this chapter tell us that we once were dead in trespasses and sins; we did what we thought was right, but found it was constantly getting us into difficulty and destroying our humanity, and we never knew why. We were victimized by the desires of the body and the mind, and were by nature, as Paul says, "children of wrath," i.e., suffering the degeneration of humanity, "like the rest of mankind."

Out of all this Christ called us. Those of us who have believed in Jesus Christ have been made alive together with him. We have become new creatures, different from anything we have ever been. Also, we have been given a new power. We have been raised up with him, so that the power upon which we are to operate is not the power of a determined will, but the power of a trusting heart, reckoning upon resurrection life. And finally, we have been given a new attitude. We have been made to sit with him in heavenly places, and have **been** allowed to relax, and be confident that God is working out his purposes in our lives. All of this conveys to us some sense of what it means to be a Christian.

In Ephesians 2:11, the Apostle takes up another view of our past life. He looks back upon what we were as pagans— *Gentiles* is the word he uses—and reminds us of our previous condition of ignorance. Not only were we dead, apart from Jesus, but we were also in the darkness of ignorance.

> Therefore remember that at one time you Gentiles in the flesh, called the uncircumcision by what is called the circumcision, which is made in the flesh by hands—remember that you were at that time separated from Christ, alienated from the commonwealth of Israel, and strangers to the covenants of promise, having no hope and without God in the world. But now in Christ Jesus you who once were far off have been brought near in the blood of Christ (Eph. 2:11–13).

In this passage the Apostle is dealing with the difference between the Jews and the Gentiles. He identifies the Gentiles for us. He says they are the ones who are called "uncircumcised" by those who are circumcised, that is, by Jewish people. He indicates that circumcision is the distinguishing mark of the Jews, and with good reason. In being circumcised they were marked out as a special people, belonging to God in a unique sense. The mark of circumcision was what indicated this distinction. So when Paul said the Jews were circumcised, he was referring to the advantages which the Jew had over the Gentile. We will see what those are shortly. But he was also highlighting the fact that the Gentiles, the pagans, did not have these advantages.

Circumcision is stressed a great deal in the Scriptures—all through the Old Testament and the New. It began, you remember, with Abraham, who circumcised his son Isaac at the request of God. It always indicated that here was a people who had a special access to God, a special relationship to him. But the Gentile world was without this.

All symbols in Scripture are very significant; they always

mean something. Why do you think God chose this sign (for God himself chose it) and placed it upon the male sex organ? Why was this part of the body chosen to be the sign of a privileged people?

Sex and Self-Image

The answer lies in the fact that we human beings are basically sexual, as the Scriptures very plainly teach. The church has often not taught this, but instead has acted as though sex were something extraneous to human beings, as though our bodies ended at the waist and we needed to be concerned about nothing further. But the Scriptures always have taught that sex is an integral part of our humanity, that we are basically and fundamentally sexual, not only at the physical level but in the soul and the spirit as well. There is a soulish form of sex, as there is a spiritual form of sex. Therefore circumcision was God's way of indicating what the Jews were to think about themselves, their self-image. How people act sexually is a dead giveaway of how they see themselves before God—in other words, their true identity.

The Gentile world was called "uncircumcised" because it was characterized primarily by two things: first, sexual immorality. The pagans of Paul's day were often highly educated —what we call "civilized"—but intermixed with their civilization was terrible sexual degeneracy. When you visit the ruins of the pagan world, the ancient temples of Rome, Greece, and other places, you invariably find a tremendous emphasis upon sex symbols. The Greek philosophers, those advanced thinkers who in many ways have never been surpassed, were nevertheless sexually degraded. Socrates, for example, involved himself in homosexual practices. Homosexuality was widely accepted and very prevalent in those days, along with many other degrading sexual practices. So, by its sexual practices, the pagan world of Paul's day revealed its lack of understanding of its own humanity.

The pagan world was also characterized by religious ignorance. They didn't know themselves, because they didn't know God. The Scriptures teach us constantly that you never know yourself until you know God. It is the knowledge of God which reveals man to himself. This is why those who have come into a knowledge of God, and grow in that knowledge, are always at the same time growing in the understanding of man and of themselves. All this is implied in the classification of the pagan world as uncircumcised: sexually aberrant, religiously ignorant.

Yet Paul gives a hint in verse 11 that the Jews, although they had many advantages over the Gentiles, were often hypocritical. They were not making use of their advantages; they were claiming what they did not actually possess. He puts it this way:

> Therefore remember that at one time you Gentiles in the flesh, called the uncircumcision by what is called the circumcision, which is made in the flesh by hands—(Eph. 2:11).

The Jews were called "circumcised," but Paul suggests here that they didn't always live as circumcised people. Circumcision was merely an outward symbol so that they were called "circumcised," though there was no corresponding inner reality.

You say, "How does this affect us? That was in the first century; here we are in the twentieth. What does this have to do with us? Gentiles may have been pagans back in Paul's day, but we don't live in that kind of world." I hope you have already realized that such is not the case. We do indeed live in that kind of world. Paganism is rampant in our day, and it is exactly the same kind of paganism as Paul had in view.

Most of us trace our ancestry to northern Europe. It is healthy for us to remember that not too many centuries ago our ancestors were wandering through the forests of northern Europe, clad in animal skins, living in caves, and were in no sense "civilized" as we define it today. Our ancestors were known to the world of Paul's day as "barbarians." And we would have remained barbarians had it not been for the influx of the gospel through brave missionaries who carried the Word to our forefathers in England and Germany and other places from which our Anglo-Saxon race has descended. It is good to remember that we would never have had what we enjoy in this country today were it not for the fact that the gospel penetrated these areas.

Let us never forget our heritage. Our fathers, who landed on the shores of New England almost four hundred years ago, were fleeing religious persecution; they were godly men and women. And we have reaped their heritage. Today many of us have been raised in a Christian environment, having come from Christian homes in a so-called "Christian" nation. We are more in the position of the Jews of Paul's day than that of the Gentiles. We have been exposed to a great deal of truth. We have many advantages, just as the Jews had. They had the potential of knowing God, but many of them did not know him. Many of us are in that condition today.

Death-Gap

Yet it is also true that many of us come right out of just such a pagan environment as Paul describes here. Let us see how he describes this condition, because it is not only the condition from which many of us come; it is also a condition toward which the world is returning as it grows more and more paganized and loses its Christian influence and teaching.

> . . . remember that you were at that time separated from Christ, alienated from the commonwealth of Israel, and strangers to the covenants of promise, having no hope and without God in the world (Eph. 2:12).

That is paganism. Paul starts at its highest possible level. The one thing which can be said of all pagans, no matter what their background, is that they are "separated from Christ." If you have not yet come to Christ, you are a pagan. You may have been brought up in a religious home. You may be trained in civilized ways. You may have been exposed to the philosophies of the world. You may be highly intelligent, very artistic, and in many ways an admirable and enjoyable person. But one great fact remains: You are separated from Christ. And without Christ you have no life from God. The

life of God is not available to you. You may know that he
exists; you may even believe in him. There were pagans in
Paul's day who did believe in God. They had turned from
the empty worship of the gods of the Greek and Roman
pantheons, believing that there was a true God somewhere.
But they didn't know him. And that is true of many today.

Paganism at the highest level is this: You are separated
from Christ. There is a gap. It may be only a small gap; you
may be close to Christ, very close. You may understand and
admire his teaching. But until you have come to know him,
until you have received him, the gap between you and him is
a death-gap. You still remain "dead in trespasses and sins," as
Paul states it in the opening verses of this chapter—following
the course of the prince of this world, fulfilling the lusts of the
passions of the flesh, a child of wrath, even as the rest of
mankind. That is the fundamental thing which can be said
of a pagan.

Paul goes on to say they were "alienated from the commonwealth of Israel." An alien is a stranger, a foreigner living in a
country without the rights of citizenship. A commonwealth is
a nation or a kingdom. Here Paul contrasts the position of the
Jews with that of the Gentiles. The Jews had a nation over
which God ruled. They gloried in the fact that God was the
head of their nation. They had a sense of destiny, a sense of
God's protection, a sense of belonging to a people who were
all under the oversight of God. They had a camaraderie, a
sense of brotherhood which came from belonging to God,
from being his people.

But the pagan world worshiped a pantheon of gods. The
Greeks had their list of gods, the Romans had theirs, the
Persians had another and the barbarians to the north—Norse-
men and others—had yet another list. All of these gods were
as irritable and as undependable as men. Pagans lived in a
world in which they were exposed to powers they recognized
as being greater than themselves, but in which there was no
consistency and never any love. Pagans never thought of God
as loving them; pagans never thought of loving God. There is
no suggestion of this in their writings at all. They never

reached out to God, never felt themselves loved by God. They could only beseech kindness and mercy of their gods, and try to influence them. But there was never a sense of belonging to God. The Jews had that sense; the pagans did not. They were aliens from the commonwealth of Israel.

You know that in time of crisis an alien is always treated differently from a citizen. When war broke out with Japan, people of Japanese ancestry on the West Coast were treated as aliens—even though most of them actually were citizens. They were suspected and interned, and no one wanted anything to do with them for a time, because they had the look of aliens. Immediately, when a crisis breaks out, this line of demarcation is very evident. Paul recognizes this of pagans. He says, "Since you weren't part of Israel, you didn't have a sense of belonging to God."

But paganism goes further than that; these were also "strangers to the covenants of promise." These covenants were the agreements God had made with Abraham and Jacob and Moses and David and others in which he bound himself to keep certain promises, if man would respond to him. Every Israelite had a hope, a way out, if he would take it. They didn't always do so, but they did have a way, if they wanted it. There were, for instance, the promises which had to do with the sacrifices. Every Israelite knew that if he were burdened with guilt, troubled by having done something wrong, there was something he could do about it: he could bring a sacrifice. God had bound himself that, if an animal were sacrificed under proper conditions, then the conscience of that individual would be eased. And furthermore, the priesthood was provided to instruct them what was right and what was wrong, what was harmful and what was harmless. And finally, there were all the promises which had to do with the Messiah. Even though the nation forgot God, turned away completely and went off and "did their own thing" like the pagans around them, yet God did not cut them off. He had promised to send a Messiah who, one day, would restore the people again. So the Jew always had the hope of the coming Messiah.

Pagan Despair

But not the pagan. This is the contrast. They had no hope in their darkness. They appeased their unreliable, irritable gods, but there was no certainty these gods would ever respond to them in any way. So when pagans were depressed or filled with guilt and shame, and they fell into violence, cruelty, and warfare which pervaded the pagan world, they had no promise of any help, no place they could turn. They had no hope in the future, but were left strictly to their own devices.

Therefore, Paul goes on, their final condition was "having no hope, and without God in the world." Archeologists have dug up first-century cemeteries in various places in Greece and Rome and have found many tombstones which bear upon them the Greek or Latin words for "No hope." In the Roman world of that day, despair reigned everywhere. If you read the writings of the Roman philosophers and thinkers of that day, you find always a philosophy of despair relating to a meaningless existence. There was little sense of purpose in life. Even the most hopeful indulged only in a kind of whistling in the dark. They looked out into the future and saw absolutely nothing significant. Their writings reveal the utter darkness, the emptiness, the hopelessness of pagan life.

You can even see this condition reflected in the Scriptures. Remember the wistful question of Pilate when Jesus told him that he had come into the world to declare the truth: Pilate responded, "What is truth?" There you can read the hopeless cynicism of an educated Roman who had learned to despair of ever finding reality. Remember the burning curiosity of the Roman proconsul, Sergius Paulus, of the island of Cyprus, when Paul and Barnabas came there. He heard about these two men, sent for them, and inquired diligently of them what this teaching was regarding Jesus. He was longing to find a way out of the hopelessness of his pagan environment.

The result, of course, is that the pagans were without God, just as Paul says. Many abandoned belief in their unde-pendable gods and became atheists. The Greek thinkers, the scientists of that day, the Roman philosophers, the statesmen, the leaders of the Roman world, looked out upon the universe and saw nothing but an enormous cosmic loneliness—just as men do today. They saw man alone in a cruel and heartless universe, struggling along, trying to do his best in his feeble way, in his brief day, with nothing lying beyond. Therefore atheism was widespread in the Roman world. We tend to assume they were all worshipping gods, but the largest proportion of the Romans and Greeks did not worship gods; they worshiped nothing. They didn't believe in gods any more. They went through the forms of worshipping, just as men do today in many churches, but there was no sense of the presence of God. To them, God was dead, just as he is to many in our day. That is paganism; it is always that way.

Someone told me recently about a project called "Cyclops," to which some brilliant scientists have devoted themselves. It involves spending large sums of money to explore the universe with telescopes and other means in an effort to discover a higher level of civilization than we know here. The only hope in their darkness is that they might possibly find a civilization which has solved some of the problems we wrestle with and, through contact with it, they might obtain remedies for the insupportable conditions of our day. That shows how pagan the world has become once more—drifting back into darkness, loneliness, hopelessness, so that men are grasping at straws, trying to find some way out of the abject despair that grips the hearts of people everywhere.

Think of that, when you think of your Christianity. Think of what it is that God has called you out of in Jesus Christ. Remember what you would have been without Christ, in the darkness of the paganism to which the world is rapidly returning.

Every now and then we are told that the ancient world was a beautiful place. It was indeed filled with great architectural achievements. We visit them as tourists and gaze in awe at the remarkable abilities of the Romans and Greeks and Persians and Mayans and others. Ah, yes. But if we could live back in those times we would see people gripped with despair, experiencing little enjoyment in life at all.

A travel folder may put before us the image of some beautiful South Sea island, where happy savages lie around indolently all day playing their ukuleles, with fish ready to be caught right at the edge of the sea, coconuts and fruit dropping off the trees, and nothing to do but enjoy life. Such folders try to call us back to the happy, primeval, simple life of these primitive people. That is complete hogwash! There never has been an idyllic society like that, and never will be. Outwardly, superficially, perhaps. But inwardly every one of them was in the grip of fear, hostility, hatred, superstition, emptiness, and religious mockery.

I read an account the other day of a South American Indian who told the missionary who led him to Christ, "When I was living in the jungle, we never knew a day without fear. When we woke up in the morning, we were afraid. When we went out of our houses, we were afraid. When we walked along the river, we were afraid. We saw an evil spirit in every stone and tree and waterfall. And when night fell, fear came into our huts and slept with us all night long." That is what paganism is. This is what the world is returning to. All around us on every side, as Christian truth begins to fade, as the nation becomes secularized and humanized, this pagan darkness settles upon the land once again.

It is true that we ought to give thanks for our Puritan fathers and the heritage they have left us. But we ought also to ask ourselves, "What are we passing on to the next generation?" Thank God there has come a degree of spiritual revival. It is wonderfully hopeful to see how young people everywhere, and older ones as well, are rediscovering the great truths of Christian faith. But how thankful it ought to make our hearts that God has given us these marvelous blessings in Jesus Christ, and has called us out of such darkness!

His Violent Death

Paul goes on now to show us what has happened:

But now in Christ Jesus you who once were far off have been brought near in the blood of Christ (Eph. 2:13).

Without Christian missionaries, without their knowledge of the Scriptures, without the instruction of those who came to know God and then brought the message to us, we would have been nothing but pagans, without any light in our darkness other than the natural light which came from our inner being, indicating that there is a God somewhere. We would be living like that still—probably in skins in caves in the woods. But now, having once been far off, we have been brought nigh by the blood of Christ, by the death of Christ.

I must point out here that it isn't merely the death of Christ which redeems. Paul says that it is specifically the *blood* of Christ. It is significant that he uses that term. Death, of course, is not always bloody. You can die without losing your blood. The Scriptures sometimes speak of the death of Christ, but more often of the cross of Christ. Yet still more often they speak of the blood of Christ. Why this emphasis? Many people today don't like to think of the cross or of the death of Jesus as being bloody. But God emphasizes it. God wants us to think about it, because blood is always a sign of violence. The death of Jesus was not just a simple passing away—dying of old age on a comfortable bed. It was a violent death, a bloody, gory, ugly, revolting scene—a man hanging torn and wretched upon a cross, with blood streaming down his sides and running down the cross.

God wants us to remember that violent death, because violence is the ultimate result of paganism. It is the final expression of a godless society. Cruelty arises immediately when love and truth disappear from society. God is simply reminding us that when humanity had done its worst, had sunk to its lowest, had vented its anger in the wretchedness and violence and blood of the cross, his love reached down to that very place and, utilizing that violent act, began to redeem, to call back those who were far off and bring them near, in the blood of Christ.

And, in the blood of Jesus, all the advantages the Jews had were conferred upon the Gentiles. Ignorant, pagan, darkened, foolish, struggling, hopeless—nevertheless, they had just as much access to God, in the blood of Christ, as any Jew ever had with his temple, his law, his priesthood, and his sacrifice. By this the Apostle is trying to emphasize to us the amazing wonder of the grace of God, which laid all our liabilities aside and reached out to us and found us just as we were, and brought us near by the blood of Jesus Christ our Lord. What a gift to give thanks for!

13

THE PRINCE OF PEACE

Ephesians 2:13–18

We come now to a section in which the Apostle Paul deals with Christ's great role as the peacemaker among men. Here we will see him in fulfillment of that prophecy in Isaiah 9: "His name will be called 'Wonderful Counselor, Mighty God, Everlasting Father, Prince of Peace'" (Isa. 9:6). This title belongs strictly to Jesus.

The secret of peace in our world seems to elude men. Paul says, in Romans, "The way of peace they do not know" (Rom. 3:17). Men don't understand what brings conflict; therefore, they cannot understand what brings peace. We can see this at the individual level, within the family circle, in a church, in a company, in a state, in a nation, and among the nations of the world. It is always the same problem: men do not know the way of peace.

In this very remarkable passage, the Apostle gives us the way of peace. He uses as an illustration the fact that Jesus Christ bridged the widest chasm which has ever existed between men—the gulf between the Jew and the Gentile. If you don't think that conflict can claim title to being the most difficult gulf to bridge, I suggest you consider why it has been so difficult to settle the Arab-Israeli problem in the Middle East. The greatest minds of our day have tried to work that out, and no one has gotten anywhere near a settlement. It is because this conflict is extremely difficult to bridge, but Paul describes how Christ actually does it. This is a wonderful picture for us of how peace can be brought in any area of conflict or hostility, whether among individuals or groups or nations. Paul says:

> But now in Christ Jesus you [Gentiles] who once were far off have been brought near in the blood of Christ. For he is our peace, who has made us both one, and has broken down the dividing wall of hostility, by abolishing in his flesh the law of commandments and ordinances, that he might create in himself one new man in place of the two, so making peace, and might reconcile us both to God in one body through the cross, thereby bringing the hostility to an end. And he came and preached peace to you who were far off and peace to those who were near; for through him we both have access in one Spirit to the Father (Eph. 2:13–18).

Paul mentions the word *peace* three times in that passage: "He is our peace," Paul says, speaking of Christ; and he has made peace (verse 15: "so making peace"); and, ". . . he came and preached peace to you who were far off and peace to those who were near." There you have the Apostle's outline of how Christ makes peace, the way he goes about it. First, he is our peace, that is, the *origin* of peace. Then he came and made peace; that is the *process* of peace. Finally, he preached peace; there is the means of laying hold or *possessing* that peace. Please understand that this is not mere doctrine, not mere theology. If you are having a conflict with anybody— whether it is in your home, at your work, in your neighborhood, in the church, or in the world, this is the way to peace. This is the secret of peace.

Is It Peace?

First, the origin of peace: "He is our peace, who has made us both one" (Eph. 2:14a). Paul starts with a definition of what true peace really is. True peace is oneness. It is not merely the cessation of hostility, the absence of conflict; it means being one. This is very important to know. Otherwise, when you talk about peace, you are only being superficial. Is it "peace" when you get two armies to lay down their weapons and stop fighting each other? Well, we call it that. And certainly it is to be preferred over armed conflict. But it is not really peace—not according to God's definition.

Is it peace when a husband and wife agree, for the sake of the children, not to get a divorce, but that home continues in coldness and divisiveness, with no harmony or joy? Well, it may be peace according to man's definition, but not according to God's. Is it peace when two friends who haven't spoken to each other for some time finally decide to agree to disagree, to speak civilly to each other, but they don't seek each other's company any more? Not according to God's definition. When a church maintains its rituals and programs, and yet is filled with division and strife and coldness and festering resentment, is that a peaceful church? No, not according to this definition.

Peace is oneness, harmony. It is sharing mutual enjoyment. It is being one. Anything else is superficial and temporary and highly unsatisfactory. If you merely agree not to fight, it is not peace. Sooner or later, a new outbreak occurs with all the previous animosity surging to the surface once again. It is only temporary, and never very satisfying. This is why what we call peace among nations never lasts—because it isn't really peace. It isn't oneness at all. It is only a weariness with warfare, an agreement to stop for awhile, until we can all recuperate and rearm. Then it breaks out all over again, because nothing is ever settled. God isn't interested in that.

But here the Apostle tells us that the secret of true peace, the secret of oneness, is a Person. "*He* is our peace." When Jesus makes peace—between individuals or between nations—that peace will be a satisfying, permanent, and genuine peace. What Paul is saying is that in order to live at peace, you must have peace. The problem with most of us is that we want to start by clearing up the results of conflict. God never starts there; he starts with the person. He says peace is a Person, and in order for you to live at peace with someone else, you must be at peace with the Person of Christ. If you have his peace, then you can start solving the conflict around you. But you can never do it on any other basis. So the place to start, the origin of peace, is to settle any problems that exist between you and Jesus Christ.

Many people come to me, as to any pastor, with various problems involving conflict. Usually they are upset, troubled, discouraged, angry. They report to me at great length all the terrible things the other person has done, and all the reasons why they are justified in being so angry and feeling so mistreated. I listen to it all, and then I have to say to them, "Yes, you've got a problem. But that isn't your only problem. You really have two problems. And the one you haven't mentioned at all is the one you must start with." Then I point out to them that their basic problem is that they don't have any peace themselves. They are not at peace. They are upset, angry, emotionally distraught. Thus everything they do and think is colored by that emotional state. They can't see anything straight, they don't see things in balance, their perspective is distorted, everything is out of focus. And it is impossible to solve the problem until they themselves acquire peace.

But such peace is the promise of God to Christians: He is our peace. And once their attitude is changed, once they have put the matter into the hands of the Lord—and their own heart is therefore at peace—then they can begin to understand what is happening and apply some intelligent remedies to the situation. There is profound psychological insight in the fact that the Apostle begins with the declaration that Christ is our peace. He alone can accomplish it, making us one.

Now look at the process of peace. How does peace come about? It comes in three stages; Paul says three things must happen before you really have oneness. This is what Christ alone can do, but this is the way he does it: First, he "has broken down the dividing wall of hostility [the hostility must end first], by abolishing in his flesh the law of commandments and ordinances." Second "that he might create in himself one new man in place of two, so making peace." And third, "might reconcile us both to God in one body through the cross, thereby bringing the hostility to an end."

On Pain of Death

I remind you that Paul is talking about the ending of the great conflict between the Jews and the Gentiles of his day. He says the first thing Jesus did was to break down the middle wall of partition, the "dividing wall of hostility." Paul is referring to a feature of the temple in Jerusalem. He was a Jew, and he understood the temple; he had been there many times. He remembered the wall, about three or four feet high, which ran through the court of the temple, separating the court of the Gentiles from the inner court into which only Jews were permitted. There was a sign on the wall which warned anyone who wasn't a Jew that if they dared to venture into this inner court, they did so on pain of death. In fact, in the year 1871, archeologists digging around the temple site in Jerusalem actually uncovered the very stone marked with this warning. These are the actual words, translated from both the Hebrew and the Greek: "No man of another race is to proceed within the partition and enclosing wall about the sanctuary. Any one arrested there will have himself to blame for the penalty of death which will be imposed as a consequence."

That wall is a symbol. It was not actually destroyed until A.D. 70, several years after this letter was written, when the temple itself was destroyed. But Paul says the hostility it represented was demolished in Jesus Christ. At best, the Jews treated the Gentiles with aloofness; at worst, they despised and hated them. There was enormous hostility between these two peoples.

Several years ago I walked along the infamous Berlin Wall. As I walked, I saw the East German guards stationed at intervals. I could feel the built-in suspicion and mutual distrust, the hatred and hostility, and the outright defiance represented by that wall. Many people have been killed trying to escape from East Germany. Where their bodies fell the West Germans have erected crosses upon which they place wreaths as a reminder, in open defiance of the East German guards. You can't enter the neighborhood of that wall without feeling the intense suspicion and hostility it represents.

There are walls like that among us. In our homes there are walls of hostility and hatred, defiance and suspicion, distrust between husbands and wives, and between parents and children. These walls of hostility arise in our relationships with friends and neighbors, as well. We feel the hostility, the anger, the deep-seated resentment and bitterness, and we say, "It's no use; there's nothing we can do." But the Apostle says that Jesus Christ knows how to remove these walls. He does this ". . . by abolishing in his flesh the law of commandments and ordinances" (Eph. 2:15). That is the way. It is the law which makes the hostility, and if you remove the law, you'll end the hostility.

Once again, we are dealing with a very profound psychological insight. The strength of any hostility is demand. The Apostle is saying that hostility is created by making a self-righteous demand upon someone, a demand without any admission of guilt on the part of the one demanding, so that it is a one-sided justice. A holier-than-thou insistence is what creates hostility. The Jews despised the Gentiles because they considered themselves better than Gentiles. "We have the law of Moses," they said. "The law is right and true; it reflects the character of God. You Gentiles don't have the law." And in their blindness and self-righteous hypocrisy they thought they were keeping this law because they didn't do some of the outward, external acts the law prohibited. So they hated and despised the Gentiles because they thought they were superior. The Gentiles, on the other hand, hated the Jews for their self-righteous hypocrisy. So there was intense hostility between them.

Jesus' solution is to end their demands on each other. Help them to see that the law judges both alike, and you'll end the hostility. Put them on the same level—they both need grace, both need forgiveness—and you remove hostility. This is so beautifully exemplified in the story in the eighth chapter of John's gospel. Jesus is confronted with a woman taken in adultery. She is dragged before him by a crowd of self-righteous Pharisees who say she has been taken in the very act. (They never mention the man who must have been involved. He gets away.) The law, they say, condemns her to death because she is guilty. And what does Jesus do? He can't deny the law. He simply stoops down and begins to write on the ground. No one knows what he wrote. I've thought that perhaps he wrote what the finger of God wrote on the wall of the palace in Babylon, when Belshazzar had his feast: *"Mene, mene, tekel, upharsin* [You have been weighed in the balances and found wanting"]. Whatever he wrote, those who watched him became convicted of their own guilt and, beginning with the eldest, John says, they began to find excuses to get away. One remembered he had an appointment; one heard his wife calling; and so they began to disappear. Finally only the woman and Jesus were left there together.

Both in the Same Bag

Now, what had Jesus done? Well, he had simply applied the law to the judges as well as to the judged. He had brought them both under the same law. He had put the judges and the judged into the same bag and shaken them up together, as a cook shakes pieces of meat in flour to coat them before cooking, and they had come out covered with the flour of guilt. There was no one left to make accusations. This is what Paul says Jesus has done with the law. He fulfilled the law in himself, and thus rendered both Jew and Gentile guilty before God. He died for them both, for both were equally guilty. When they learned of his bloody death as an innocent substitute, the Jews knew they were just as guilty as the Gentiles. Paul argues at great length in Romans 2 through 4 that the Jew has no advantage at all over the Gentile simply because he knows more truth, but he stands on exactly the same ground—Jew and Gentile need to be forgiven. So our Lord gave them a common ground of forgiveness, and when he did, there was no hostility left.

The way to end hostility, then, is to end self-righteousness. Remove the self-righteousness, the demand that your friend change without admitting your own need for change. As long as you insist that he is all wrong, and there is nothing at all you need to change, then of course, hostility and resentment remain. I've seen this method work with parents and children. As long as parents insist they never make mistakes, never do anything wrong, never need to apologize, never say "I'm sorry" to their children, those children invariably grow up resenting and hating their parents. Self-righteousness always creates hostility. It is only when parents see themselves as able to be wrong, needing forgiveness themselves, needing to be understood and set free by the forgiveness of their children, as well as granting forgiveness to them, that there can be harmony. I've seen the same principle work between friends, and among church leaders and other Christians. Hostility comes by self-righteous demand. Remove that demand, and the hostility ends.

Then what? Is God content merely to end hostility? Never. There is a second step, ". . . that he might create in himself one new man" (Eph. 2:15). Notice the word *create*. Only God can create. When we say of somebody, "He's creative," we mean he is able to take things which are already there and put them together in a new way, thus bringing about something different. He has rearranged the material, and we call that creativity. But in the ultimate sense of the word, only God is creative. Men may be ingenious, but they're not creative. Only God can create something out of nothing. He makes a new man, a new unity which never existed before.

Many people have experienced this. People often say to me, "You know, since I stopped trying to judge my husband (or my wife), and we've come together acknowledging that we both need God, both need forgiveness, I've discovered that we have a whole new relationship I never dreamed was possible. It is better than anything we had before." Something new has begun, a greater unity than ever has developed. Sometimes people come to me and say, "Our marriage is dead. Our love is gone. There's no way we can restore it. We might as well end the marriage." It is a great joy to point out to them that in Christ a new relationship comes into being, something which never was there before. Many have laid hold of this and found it indeed to be true that in the new unity, "the new man" which grows out of the relationship brought to Christ, there is a freedom and a glory and a beauty and a richness which was never there before.

Here in Ephesians, of course, "the new man" Paul refers to is the church itself, which is a picture of what Jesus Christ does. In the church there is neither Jew nor Gentile. The Jew does not have to become a Gentile; the Gentile does not have to become a Jew; but both are to be Christian. There is a *new* man; a new person is created. And the same is true of any other division among men. Blacks don't have to become whites, and whites don't have to become blacks in the church. Both can bring their own distinctive cultural heritage to the church, and they don't have to give it up. In that sense, the church is never to integrate; it is to make a new man. They both bring what they are, and they discover that there is a oneness, a fellowship, a union, a beautiful relationship which ultimately has nothing to do with cultural heritage. There is a sense of belonging to one another, and a joy in that relationship. The same is true of the poor and the rich. The poor don't have to live like the rich; the rich don't have to live like the poor. There can be different standards of living within the church, but there is a oneness and a joy and an acceptance of one another. The same is true between male and female. Males don't have to be female; females don't have to act like males. In the church there is a oneness. A new unity is formed which cannot be discovered apart from the settling of hostility on the ground of the peace that Jesus Christ gives.

There is still a third step: ". . . and might reconcile us both to God in one body through the cross" (Eph. 2:16a). In other words, ultimate peace must be with God. Once the hostility has been ended by the removal of a self-righteous demand and we have begun to experience this new unity in Christ, we must see ourselves as being forgiven and accepted by God. Otherwise, self-righteousness will begin to arise again, sooner or later. If there is any area in which one feels superior to the other, in which one says, "I didn't need quite as much forgiveness as that one did; my level of life was higher," then self-righteousness starts in again. But if they stand before God on the same level, on the same ground exactly, both needing the same forgiveness, then the hostility is brought to an end. This is what the Apostle says, ". . . thereby bringing the hostility to an end" (Eph. 2:16b)—a complete and total end.

Just as Much in Need

A few months ago I was in another city, and a young man came up to me and said, "I want to tell you about my marriage. I haven't been married very long. After we were married I discovered that my wife was not a virgin before we were married, though I was. I had a tremendous struggle with this. I forgave her; I understood the situation, understood that she needed to be forgiven. But emotionally I continued to wrestle. Then I began to see that my behavior had been no better than hers, before God. Though she violated the external precepts of sexual morality, I had violated them also, internally, in my thoughts and attitudes. And, before God, there was no difference. I began to see that I was just as much in need of forgiveness for my failures as she was. When I saw that, then there was healing."

This is what Paul is saying. We are to see each other as no different whatsoever, before God. If in one area of our life we think we have never done wrong, in that area we are totally unacceptable to God. The only ground we have to stand on before him is that of forgiveness, and "not of works, lest any man should boast" (Eph. 2:9). Therefore, everyone stands before God on the same level. When people see this, hostility is brought to an end. Nobody is pointing a finger, nobody is blaming the other, nobody is saying, "Well, if only you'd done this, then I could have done that." All such division and schism and hostility is brought to an end, and there is only the reception of the grace and the forgiveness of God. Hearts are healed, and hostility ends.

In the last section, Paul sets before us the means of possessing peace. How do we actually lay hold of peace?

And he came and preached peace to you who were far off and peace to those who were near; for through him we both have access in one Spirit to the Father (Eph. 2:17–18).

Two steps are necessary to lay hold of this kind of peace. The first is believing the message God has given you. "He came and preached peace," says Paul to these Ephesians. That is, "Jesus preached to you." How did he do it? He didn't come in person; he came in the person of Paul. Paul was sent by the Lord. That is what the word *apostle* means, "sent one." Paul says in 2 Corinthians, "We beseech you on behalf of Christ [in the place of Christ], be reconciled to God" (2 Cor. 5:20). Paul's preaching was Jesus' preaching of peace. Christ seized the initiative and sent the Apostle to proclaim the fact which God had already brought into being. All that remains is to believe it. When you believe that the ground of self-righteousness has been removed, that you have no more standing before God because of what you think has been proper behavior than somebody who has failed openly and blatantly, then you have begun to believe what God has said. You have begun to believe the preaching of peace. Preaching is never an argument, never a debate or dialogue. Preaching is simply the announcement of a fact. You can either accept it or reject it, but you can't quarrel with it. It is what God says is true. And this is what God says is true: that the ground of self-righteousness has been removed, and a new relationship will come into being which will be better and more beautiful, richer than anything you've known before. And God says he is satisfied with the arrangement, that he accepts you both on those terms.

The Closest Possible Relationship

Then what? Well, the last step is beautiful. It is communication with the Father: ". . . through him [the Son] we both have access in one Spirit to the Father" (Eph. 2:18).

You can come before him, upheld by the mystery of the entire Trinity at work on your behalf. This is probably the greatest statement in the book of Ephesians. I don't know a higher plateau of truth than this. There is the Trinity of God—Father, Son, and Holy Spirit—all working together to bring us into the closest possible relationship with God: the understanding and the daily experience of his fatherhood, his fatherly care over us. So we begin to understand that the circumstances of our life are chosen by the Father, that the trials and pressures and joys and sorrows all have been selected by a loving Father. We begin to see that his provision of power and truth and life is all available in Jesus Christ, and we understand that we can appeal to him. We can cry out to him. He invites us to communicate with him, to unload before him all the burdens and pressures of our life.

There is nothing higher than this. When the full glory of this relationship with the Father breaks upon us, we will have discovered that nothing can be greater. "This is eternal life," Jesus said, "that they know thee the only true God, and Jesus Christ whom thou hast sent" (John 17:3). We've been climbing with Paul, step by step, up a great mountain. And now we have come to the very summit: "For through him we both have access in one Spirit to the Father" (Eph. 2:18). We can go no higher. Life with the Father is the most delightful of all experiences, for all that we need is provided by a Father's heart, and a Father's love. This is the way God deals with us and our hostility. What separates us from each other is our insistence that they are wrong and we are right, that there is never any reason for an admission of guilt on our part. But as soon as we admit that we are wrong in the very areas where we think we are right, and that there is no way of justifying ourselves before God in any area of our lives other than being forgiven, then the hostility ends; and God brings us into that glorious relationship of freedom and enjoyment of life with the Father.

Our holy Father, we thank you for the access we have to you, our loving heavenly Father. We thank you that you accept us, enjoy us, glory in us, and are tenderly concerned about the most intimate details of our needs. Father, how foolish we have often been, to stand in self-righteous judgment against others. Father, forgive us for that. How like that unrighteous steward we have often been, when we have been forgiven so much, but have been unwilling to extend forgiveness to another. Awaken us, Lord, to the great debt we have before you. Help us to believe the message of peace which has been preached, to understand the announcement of the Holy Spirit to our hearts, and thus to enter into the joy of life with you. We ask in Jesus' name, Amen.

14

THE THIRD RACE

Ephesians 2:19–22

The title of this chapter is not a reference to an event at the race track, but is an actual description of early Christians by a pagan contemporary in the first century. Every nationality tends to divide the world into two parts—them and us. The Jews always looked upon the world of their day as made up of Jews and Gentiles. Anyone not a Jew was a Gentile in the eyes of the Jewish people. The Greeks did the same. The Greeks were the "civilized" people, and all the rest were "barbarians." The word *barbarian* comes from *barbar*, which means "to stammer." Anyone who didn't speak Greek, the civilized language, sounded to the Greeks like a stuttering child. When the Romans took over the Greek civilization, they adopted the same terminology. Everyone within the Roman Empire was Roman; all others were barbarians. The Chinese did the same thing. *China* is derived from their word for "middle"; they saw themselves as the center of the earth, the Middle Kingdom. Everyone else lived out on the periphery of the earth.

The Apostle Paul adopts this terminology in writing to the Ephesian Christians. He points out to them that they began either as Jews or Gentiles—one or the other—and that this division reflected their relationship to God. The Jews were near to God. They had the Scriptures, they had the promises, they had knowledge of God and contact with him; therefore they were close, near at hand. The Gentiles were far-off. They were pagans, living in superstitious fear, with a hopeless outlook on life. Both were separated from God. Both needed to take the final step which would actually bring them to God through Jesus Christ. And, as we have just seen, in Christ both Jew and Gentile are made one. A new unity is created, a "third race," something different than ever existed before. This change takes place before God, so that it is a realistic and permanent entity.

In the passage we come to now, the Apostle goes on to give us the advantages and privileges which are a product of this new unity in Jesus Christ between Jew and Gentile. Here we learn more about the tremendous resources which are ours as Christians. So many people are wrestling with terrible anxieties, fears, and hostilities which actually prevent them from acting as God intended human beings to act, all because they have not discovered the full resources which are available in Jesus Christ. The Apostle labored continually to set these before his readers by direct statement or, as in this case, with certain figures or pictures, so that we might understand more fully.

> So then you are no longer strangers and sojourners, but you are fellow citizens with the saints and members of the household of God, built upon the foundation of the apostles and prophets, Christ Jesus himself being the cornerstone, in whom the whole structure is joined together and grows into a holy temple in the Lord; in whom you also are built into it for a dwelling place of God in the Spirit (Eph. 2:19–22).

Notice that three beautiful figures are employed in this passage, following one upon the other, and each is an advance upon the previous one. These are designed to teach us great truths about what it means to be a Christian. There is the figure of a kingdom ("fellow citizens with the saints"), a family ("members of the household of God"), and a building ("a holy temple . . . for a dwelling place of God in the Spirit"). These are designed to instruct us so that Paul's prayer for us in the first chapter will be answered. His prayer was,

". . . having the eyes of your hearts enlightened, that you may know what is the hope to which he has called you, what are the riches [the enriching possibilities] of his glorious inheritance in the saints, and what is the immeasurable greatness of his power in us who believe . . ." (Eph. 1:18–19). We must learn to take these words literally and plainly and personally, so that we will understand what to do when we get into difficulty, how to handle problems, and how to work out relationships which are strained or broken. It is with his great resources that we can solve these problems

Strangers No More

Now let us take a closer look at the passage. Notice that the Apostle begins with a negative. "You Ephesians," he says "are no longer strangers and sojourners." That is, "Once you were strangers and [literally] foreigners, but now no longer." What is a stranger? We have all been strangers at one time or another. We have come into a city or a state which is different from our own and haven't known where to go or what to do because we were ignorant of the resources of the community. A stranger is characterized by not knowing much about the place where he is. He is ignorant of the advantages of this community, of all the cultural possibilities, of where the finest stores are located. Once we were strangers, says the Apostle. We did not know what God could do for us. We had no idea of the resources of peace and joy and forgiveness. We knew nothing of his capacity for handling our pride and our phobias and our hostilities. But no more, he says; now that we have come to Christ we are strangers no more.

And we are no longer foreigners, either. A foreigner is different from a stranger. A foreigner may be very familiar with the country in which he lives; he may have lived there for years. But he is limited because he is an alien; he has no ultimate rights. He is living on a passport. He does not have a birth certificate which makes him a citizen of that land.

This is descriptive of many people in churches. They attend church regularly, and often study the Bible, and are familiar with the hymns. Perhaps they have been raised in a

Christian family, and the language of Christianity is very familiar to them, but they have never become a Christian. They are foreigners, living on a passport. In a time of crisis aliens are deported or confined; they are not permitted to enter into the full rights of citizens of the land. But Paul says that you who have come to Christ are no longer strangers and foreigners.

Well, then, what are you? First, you are "fellow citizens with the saints." That great phrase captures the idea of a new kingdom—you have changed your citizenship and are now under another authority. Most of us take the rights of American citizenship so much for granted that we have almost forgotten the responsibilities of citizenship and the fact that we are under authority. The government has certain powers over us, regulating certain areas of our life, whether we like it or not. We are under certain controls, and if we do certain things the government can step in and actually take our freedom from us. We are under authority—that is the first mark of citizenship.

Citizens of Another Kingdom

The Bible recognizes two kingdoms in this world. In addition to the nations of earth, with their temporal authority, there are two spiritual kingdoms, and each of us belongs to one or the other. It is either the kingdom of Satan or the kingdom of God which has ultimate dominion over our lives. When you become a Christian, you move out of the kingdom of Satan into the kingdom of God, and what a change this is! It is a basic change of government, of the ultimate rule in your life. Jesus often spoke of the kingdom he came to bring among men. He said, "I am a king, but my kingdom is not of this world," (John 18:36), by which he meant that it is not like any of the nations of earth. His kingship is within the hearts of men. But it *is* a kingdom; it has authority over men. When we come into his kingdom, we come under a new authority, a new king, a new head. We are no longer under the bondage and power of the other.

Since we are citizens of another kingdom, even while we

are still here on earth, there are certain responsibilities and privileges given to us in Christ which we must learn about. Just as every American citizen must study American history in order to understand his country and what has happened in the past, so we must learn the history of this great kingdom of God in order to understand why we have certain privileges.

When I travel abroad I am always glad that I am an American citizen. I know there is much in the history of our country which is to be regretted, but every nation has had similar problems. No nation I know of has done more to benefit the other peoples of earth. So I rejoice in the great privileges which are mine as an American citizen. I am granted the use of certain resources which other nationalities cannot enjoy. Protection is extended to me as an American citizen which others do not have.

We have something similar in the kingdom of God. We have the protection of the King, and we have the right to expect him to protect us. There is power available—resurrection power, the kind that works beyond human thinking and planning. And God invites us to call upon him for that kind of resource, that kind of deliverance, whenever we need it. Jesus said, in effect, "When people persecute you, rejoice and be glad, because your King has not forgotten you, and there is a great reward laid up for you." He knows what to do. Furthermore, "Vengeance is mine, I will repay, says the Lord" (Rom. 12:19). "Don't try to work it out on your own," he says, "I have not forgotten. I know how to straighten things out, and to do so in such a way that you will ultimately be glad and not ashamed. I am not merely going to move in and crack heads together; I'm going to solve the problem in a way that will be permanently peaceful." So we have access to the King, and we can expect his protection and his justice.

Supper with Abraham

And as Paul points out here also, we share in a tremendous glory; we are fellow citizens with the *saints*. Who are these saints he is mentioning? As Paul writes, he is thinking of the great saints of the Old Testament, men like Abraham and Moses, Elijah and Elisha, David, Isaiah, and Jeremiah. We have an inheritance with them; we belong to the same kingdom. As Americans, many of us are proud that we belong to the nation which produced George Washington, Abraham Lincoln, and other great men. Here is an association like that. We will actually become personal friends with men such as Abraham, Moses, David, Daniel and Noah. Jesus himself said, "I tell you, many will come from east and west and sit at table with Abraham, Isaac, and Jacob in the kingdom of heaven" (Matt. 8:11). Think of that! What a tremendous privilege to know these people whom God has honored in the past—Paul and Peter and James and John, Luther and Augustine and Wesley. We have often sung the hymns of Charles Wesley and his brother John. There will be a day when we will sit down with "Chuck" and "Jack" Wesley and talk with them about what they've been doing. This is the intimacy of the kingdom of God, of being "fellow citizens with the saints." Together, we have access to the King himself, which is the most marvelous privilege of all.

In the second figure we are called "members of the household of God." This is an advance beyond the first. We are all citizens of the kingdom, if we are in Christ. We belong to God's kingdom, that spiritual kingdom which rules over all the nations of earth, and ultimately will be the winner in all of history. But more than that, says the Apostle, we are members of God's own intimate family. John the Apostle could never get over this. He said, "See what love the Father has given us, that we should be called children of God; and so we are" (1 John 3:1). Children of the living God! You can see what an advance this is. A child always outranks any ambassador or governor or secretary or minister or senator. I once read a biography of Abraham Lincoln that related an incident which occurred during the Civil War when the President was involved with his Cabinet in a very crucial meeting. They were in the Cabinet room working out their grand strategy when there came a knock at the door. There stood little Willie, the President's ten-year-old son, wanting to see his father for a moment. Abraham Lincoln laid aside all the duties of state and left the Cabinet members cooling their heels, while he saw what Willie wanted. Willie outranked all the others. He had access to his father. This is the great truth that Paul is trying to bring home to our hearts—the fact that we have access to a Father, a Father who is the King, with tremendous authority and power in the affairs of the world, in life as it is lived right now.

The provision and protection of a father is always more intimate and personal even than that of a king. A king is concerned about our general welfare, but a father wants to know all about our intimate problems. Is this not what Jesus teaches? He says again and again, "Don't you know that your heavenly Father knows that you have need of these things? He even knows the number of the hairs of your head." Your Father's concern is all around you, about every aspect of your life. He is not only concerned about getting justice for you. A king does that. But you are the object of his deepest, most intimate, personal concern. As Zechariah tells us about God that anyone "who touches you touches the apple of his eye" (Zech. 2:8). Could anything be closer than that?

The Most Intimate Relationship

Yes, there is something. Paul goes on, in the third figure, to an even closer relationship: You are "built upon the foundation of the apostles and prophets, Christ Jesus himself being the cornerstone" (Eph. 2:20). Perhaps that seems something of an anticlimax. After all, a building is rather cold and impersonal compared with the relationship of a family. But if you look carefully you will see what is in the Apostle's mind. He is actually moving closer, higher, to a more intimate relationship, because he is stressing the closeness of the members of the habitation of God—to one another and to the Lord. It is possible for the members of a family to be scattered throughout the earth. You may have family members who are thousands of miles away. You are still related, still members one of another, but you are widely separated and haven't seen one another for years. But, in the figure of a building, no separation of stones which make up the walls is possible. Everything is closely joined together, knit together. If the stones were separated, the building would crumble. So the Apostle is really considering a much more intimate relationship.

Furthermore, he says that this building is a living, growing habitation of God. The figure of a building merges right into the figure of a body. The building becomes the body of God, the dwelling place where God himself lives. And what could be more personal, more intimate to you than your body? We reserve the word *intimate* for that which concerns our body. An intimate relationship is one which touches you physically, touches your body. Thus Paul is reminding us of how close we are to God—a God of power, a God of might, a God of love—of how intimate his relationship is to us. He ties us all together, building us into this tremendous temple in which he himself has chosen to live.

Paul mentions that we are built on the foundation of the apostles and the prophets—the men who first disseminated the Christian faith, beyond our Lord himself. They are the foundation. Their faith and their teaching is what we rest upon. They taught us that Jesus was Lord, but the Spirit of God taught them this.

I have often thought that those who had the most difficulty of all in believing that Jesus was God must have been his own disciples. Imagine them as they walk with him and talk with him and see his humanity. They listen to him laughing and breathing, watch him sleeping and perhaps even snoring, see him subject to the normal limitations of human life, even going through the normal elimination processes, like everyone else. How difficult it must have been for them to grasp the great fact that here was God the Son, become flesh. Yet they came to this knowledge. John says:

And the Word became flesh and dwelt among us, full of grace and truth; we have beheld his glory, glory as of the only Son from the Father (John 1:14).

They examined him intimately; for three and a half years they lived closely with him. And there came at last the conviction that here indeed was God, living in human flesh. He was God, yet fully manifesting what humanity was to be like. And so on their faith we rest. They taught us the truth about the Lord Jesus. Their faith and teaching is the foundation of our faith.

But, the Apostle says, Christ himself is the chief cornerstone. When you build a building, you place the cornerstone; and all the measurements of the building are taken from that cornerstone. Everything relates to it. The whole building ties together because of the cornerstone. The Apostle depicts Jesus as having that relationship with us. You notice that all through this letter he cannot forget him for a second. Everything is "in Christ," "in him," "by him," "through him," "through his blood," "by his death." Everything comes to us in Christ. If you do not have Jesus, there is no way you can have intimate fellowship with God. "No one comes to the Father but by me" (John 14:6). So it is all built on Christ. He is the great cornerstone of our faith. And yet we are all members of it, stones being joined together.

Knocking Off the Rough Edges

Some years ago I helped a missionary friend build his house in northern Mexico, among the Tarahumara Indians. He had hired an Indian stonemason to work on the walls, and I was very interested to watch him. He had a pile of stones he had dug up and gathered in from the hillside. He would go and look at these stones and pick one he thought was the right size and shape. Then he would take a chisel and hammer and knock off a piece here and smooth off an edge there, and then place it where he wanted it to go. If it didn't quite fit, he would knock off another piece here and there until it was exactly right. Then he would cement it in place with mortar. That is exactly the picture Paul has given us here of how God works with us. He is knocking off the rough edges, shaping us up, getting us ready. If he has put you with some people you don't like, it is because they are the chisel he is using to knock off some rough edges. This is no joke; it is exactly what God is doing. He is building a temple, a holy temple, a beautiful, magnificent building.

I know nothing which makes any sense of history except this point of view. If we read history apart from this outlook we have nothing but a meaningless jumble of political campaigns and battles and bloodshed among warring factions. But if you look at history from this point of view you will see that every one of those battles, every one of those campaigns, was part of the process of God—preparing his people, straightening them out, chiseling a piece here, chipping a piece there, sanding them down, smoothing them out, getting them ready, building them in, fitting them in place in this great temple. One day the only thing left of history will be this temple God has built, the Church of Jesus Christ. Everything else—all our great buildings, all our vaunted progress—will have been lost in the dust of some nuclear storm. The only thing left will be the Church of Jesus Christ, the people in whom God dwells.

When the temple of Solomon was built, we read in 1 Kings 6:7:

> . . . it was with stone prepared at the quarry; so that neither hammer nor axe nor any tool of iron was heard in the temple, while it was being built.

It was a quiet, secret process. Stones were shaped down in the quarry, and then brought up to be fitted into place without the sound of a hammer. This is a beautiful picture of what God is doing with the Church of Jesus Christ today. Already we are temples of the living God. Individually, our bodies are the temple of God himself. How great will be our resources when we understand how closely God has knit us to himself, making us his dwelling place, and giving us full access to him as our King and our Father.

Our heavenly Father, our eyes are so often dull and dim.
We so often take these figures as though they were mere

words on paper. We pray that you will help us to see the living reality behind them, to see what you are doing in our lives, how you have chosen us and selected us to be stones, part of this living building which is growing together; and how we are to belong to each other and draw closer to one another, that we might fulfill your great purpose in having a place to live, a dwelling place of God. Our Father, help us to remember all this in times of personal difficulty, to remember how you are a Father, a great King, and that we have privileges and rights and access and resources that many of us have never even claimed. Help us now to live in the fullness of the provision you have made for us, not only as servants but as sons of the living God. We ask this, and thank you, in Jesus' name, Amen.

15

THE GREAT MYSTERY

Ephesians 3:1–6

We all love mysteries. We are fascinated by any hidden, secret, cryptic truth which needs to be discovered and revealed. God understands us so thoroughly that he has hidden mystery in everything in life. We do not know anything fully; there is always an element we don't understand. Even terms we commonly use, such as *love* and *joy* and *life,* are basically mysterious to us. We know they are absolutely essential to our existence, but we don't know what they are. We struggle constantly trying to understand the great realities they represent. Physicists tells us that mystery is hidden away in every physical manifestation of the world and universe around us. The quantum theory, upon which much of modern physics is based and which has opened up the whole realm of nuclear fission, has at its heart a hidden principle of indeterminism. It states that we can never discover the whole truth about anything; there is an element of hidden information about every subject we go into. It is mystery which makes life entrancing, fascinating. And God understands this, which is why the Scriptures say, "It is the glory of God to conceal things, but the glory of kings is to search things out" (Prov. 25:2). God knows that we all want to be kings, that we are made to reign. And the glory of kings is to discover that which has been hidden.

The Apostle Paul describes the greatest mystery of life in these words:

> For this reason I, Paul, a prisoner for Christ Jesus on behalf of you Gentiles—assuming that you have heard of the stewardship of God's grace that was given to me for you, how the mystery was made known to me by revelation, as I have written briefly. When you read this you can perceive my insight into the mystery of Christ, which was not made known to the sons of men in other generations as it has now been revealed to his holy apostles and prophets by the Spirit; that is, how the Gentiles are fellow heirs, members of the same body, and partakers of the promise in Christ Jesus through the gospel (Eph. 3: 1–6).

There, in very brief form, is his statement of the mystery which lies at the heart of all life. As we will see, this is the greatest secret ever presented to the minds of men. It is not new to us—we have been discussing and discovering aspects of it all along in this letter. But now we come to the full statement of what it is. The paragraph falls very simply into two divisions: Paul is concerned first about his role as a teacher of this mystery, and then about the mystery itself.

Sometimes it is difficult to see how Paul builds his letters. This is particularly true of this passage, because Paul begins, "For this reason. . . ." But he doesn't give the reason toward which he is moving until verse 13. This is the way the Apostle's mind worked. He starts out to say one thing but then is captured by the truth of something else he is going to say, so he brings it in ahead of time. Then he is carried along from one truth to another until he finally gets back to what he started to say in the beginning. If you read it this way: "For this reason . . ." then skip down to verse 13: ". . . I ask you not to lose heart over what I am suffering for you, which is your glory," you will understand what he is trying to say in the intervening sentences.

The Apostle was concerned that the Christians to whom he was writing at this time in his life—the Ephesians, Philippians, and others—would understand why he was going through the struggles he had. If you and I had been in Rome with Paul as he wrote this letter and could have stood in the room of the hired house where he was living, chained day and night to a Roman soldier; if we could have watched as he dictated to his amanuensis, his secretary, pacing the floor, perhaps, with the soldier having to walk along with him, we would have understood something of Paul's concern for the recipients of this letter. They could not comprehend why the mighty Apostle had to be a prisoner—limited, unable to come to them in their need as a growing young church—and why all communication with him had to be by correspondence. So he was writing to settle their fears and to show them what it was all about.

Not Caesar's Prisoner

His first statement is this: "I am a prisoner for Christ Jesus on behalf of you Gentiles." That is the first thing he wants them to know. It is striking that nowhere does Paul ever refer to himself as a prisoner of Caesar. He *was* Caesar's prisoner. He had been arrested because he was charged by the Jews with sedition, or treason, against the emperor. Therefore, eventually, he was remanded to the care of the palace guard, the personal bodyguard of the emperor. So here he was in Rome, a prisoner of Caesar, awaiting trial before Nero. But never once does he say that he is a prisoner of Caesar; it is always "a prisoner of Christ Jesus."

The reason is obvious when you read his letters. He saw that Caesar was not the one who had the final say about him; Jesus did. The duration of his confinement was not determined by Caesar but by the Lord Jesus. As Paul came to understand the One whom he served, he knew that Jesus is in control of history. He saw him as John did in the book of Revelation—sitting on his throne, holding the reins of government in his hands. He is the One who opens, and no man shuts who shuts, and no man opens who orders, and his will is carried out. Paul knew, therefore, that any time the Lord Jesus decided Paul's imprisonment would be of no further value he would be set free, and that when the Lord Jesus spoke, Caesar acted. Therefore, he never saw himself as the prisoner of Caesar. This is a tremendous lesson to us, who sometimes become worried and anxious about what today's political powers are doing in the world. Would that we had the faith of this mighty Apostle who understood so clearly that Caesar was not in control; Jesus is.

Then Paul cites some reasons for his imprisonment. First, he was a prisoner on behalf of the Gentiles. This means that his arrest had come about because he was preaching the gospel to the Gentiles. Do not forget that the reason the Jews charged Paul with sedition against the emperor was that they were angry that he would carry any message from God to the Gentiles. Jewish scruples and prejudices were terribly offended by the fact that Paul had the nerve, the effrontery, to say to the Jews that the Gentiles could have equal standing with the Jews before God. When Paul spoke to the Jewish mob in his own defense, after he was arrested in the temple courts, the thing which triggered their renewed ire was the word *Gentiles* in his message. They had been listening carefully to him as he spoke of his conversion, of how he had been called by God, but when he stated that he had been sent out to the Gentiles, all hell broke loose again. They mobbed him and would have lynched him on the spot had it not been for the intervention of the Roman guard. So it was because of this great message that he was a prisoner.

But also, he wants these Ephesians to know that they were benefiting by his arrest. I think this is a hint that he recognized that if he had not been made a prisoner he would never have had the time to write these letters which have changed the course of history. His concern for these people was such that he would have gone to them had he been free. He would have preached to them and taught them directly from the Word, but would never have found time to write it down. So perhaps the reason the Lord Jesus kept him a prisoner was so he might have time to write. He may have to do that with some of us, too. You may have learned truth you ought to write down and pass along. Have you ever thought of that possibility? Writing these letters is the greatest thing the Apostle ever did, for it is these which have changed our lives. And he recognizes that they were written on behalf of the Gentiles.

The second thing Paul says about himself, to help them understand what he was going through, is that he was a steward of God's grace. God had committed a certain responsibility to him. I'm glad the Revised Standard Version uses the translation "stewardship" instead of "dispensation," for *dispensation* is often misunderstood in our day. But if we see it as a stewardship we will understand it. A steward was a servant to whom a certain responsibility was committed, certain goods were given, so that he might "dispense" them, give them out to other people. This is the biblical idea behind the word *dispensation*. It is not a period of time at all; it is a responsibility to dispense something, a stewardship. That is what Paul said was given to him. He was a responsible steward. This is exactly in line with what he had written to the Corinthians much earlier.

> This is how one should regard us [apostles], as servants of Christ and stewards of the mysteries of God (1 Cor. 4:1).

The "mysteries" are the sacred secrets that God knows about life, which men desperately need to know. Think of this! Paul says we Christians—beginning with apostles, and including everyone who names the name of Christ—are stewards, responsible servants, given the responsibility of dispensing the mysteries of God, of helping people understand these great secrets which explain life and make it possible to solve the difficulties and problems of our human affairs. This responsibility has been committed to us, and this is how Paul sees himself—as a steward of the mysteries of God.

The Apostle's Authority

And, more than this, he was personally taught about God's grace by none other than the Lord Jesus himself—". . . it came through a revelation of Jesus Christ" (Gal. 1:12). This is where we get our understanding of the authority of this

great Apostle. There are those who tell us that the Apostle
Paul learned his gospel from the other apostles, who in turn
had heard it from Jesus, and that therefore Paul's Apostle-
ship is somewhat inferior to theirs. But Paul says this is not
true. He tells us very plainly in his letter to the Galatians
that when he was converted on that Damascus road, "I did
not receive it from any man, nor was I taught it, but it came
through a revelation of Jesus Christ" (Gal. 1:12). He didn't
talk with the other apostles; in fact, it was three years before
he ever went back to Jerusalem after his conversion. And
then he saw only James, the Lord's brother, and Peter, and
they didn't talk about doctrine. It wasn't until fourteen years
later that he ever had an opportunity to sit down and compare notes with all the other apostles. When he did, he says,
"they added nothing to me." He understood everything they
did, knew everything Jesus had taught them in the days of
his flesh.

A striking example of this is found in 1 Corinthians, where
he writes about the Lord's Supper. He says, "For I received
from the Lord what I also delivered to you, that the Lord
Jesus on the night when he was betrayed took bread, and
when he had given thanks, he broke it, and said, 'This is my
body which is for you. Do this in remembrance of me'"
(1 Cor. 11:23–24). This means that Jesus himself had appeared to Paul and had told him all that went on in the upper room. So when Peter and James and John and the other
apostles began to compare notes with Paul, they were aston-
ished that this man who had been the persecutor of the
church and the chief murderer of the saints in Jerusalem,
understood not only the doctrine they had been taught, but
also the very events they had gone through. Thus they had to
acknowledge that he was an apostle on equal terms with
them. This is what gives Paul his authority.

Every now and then we run across someone who says,
usually in defense of Women's Liberation, that Paul was a
crusty old bachelor whom no one can really trust, that we
must understand that he was conditioned by the culture of
his time and therefore, one must pick and choose among his

writings as to what to believe. Paul himself, and all the other apostles, would deny this. Here was a man who spoke with direct authority, commissioned by the Lord Jesus himself.

Paul says here that he has "written briefly" about this revelation already. Scholars are not exactly sure what he meant by that. Some feel that he had written another letter before this, which had explained much of this mystery. But I think it is a reference to what he has written previously in this letter. In Ephesians 1:9–10 he says:

> For he [God the Father] has made known to us in all wisdom and insight the mystery of his will, according to his purpose which he set forth in Christ as a plan for the fulness of time, to unite all things in him, things in heaven and things on earth.

That is the brief statement he had written to these Ephesian Christians and to which he refers. Now he continues, "When you read this you can perceive my insight into the mystery of Christ" (Eph. 3:4). That is, "You can understand that I have great grasp and understanding of what this mystery is, that it is really the secret of all things, touching everything in life. It is at the heart of all human existence. It is the mystery of the goal toward which God is moving in human affairs; therefore it encompasses space, time, matter— all of life." And he sums it up in these words: *the mystery of Christ*—Jesus Christ, at the heart of all things.

All Puzzles Solved Here

None of us can help but be aware that this is an extremely troubled time in which we are living. We do not know how to solve the problems which are overwhelming us. We are being swamped by our own inventions. We continue to make automobiles even after they have glutted the highways and poisoned the air. We don't know how to break loose from this syndrome. We don't know what to do with the millions of people who have been shoved off into ghettos, the impoverished areas of our cities where economic pressures force them to live. We don't know how to feed the world. We are

unable to stem the tide of broken marriages, and so our
divorce rate is higher than that of any other nation in the
world.

Many writers—thoughtful, perceptive men—are sitting
down and trying to analyze where we have gone wrong, and
why we cannot understand what to do. Some propose one
solution and some another; some are partially right, and some
are almost totally wrong. But the reason they cannot grasp
the answer is that they have never dealt with the heart of
the problem, the great secret to all things. That key mystery
is Christ, says the Apostle.

If you think that is merely theological language, you have
missed the import of what he is saying: Every problem of life
finds its final solution in the Person and Being of the Lord
Jesus himself. God has set his Son at the heart of all things.
Therefore the understanding of this great mystery is the key
to the ultimate solutions for which men are seeking today. If
we understand who Christ is, what he does, and how we can
lay hold of him, we will begin to see the solutions of these
problems unfold, as they are indeed unfolding in many of our
lives. Solutions come into being as we grasp what Christ has
made available to us. I know that sometimes we are so
blinded by familiarity with these terms that we miss the impact. But I pray that God will open the eyes of your understanding, that you will see how fantastic is this great mystery,
and how important it is to understand it thoroughly, and to
enter into it.

When Einstein discovered his theory of relativity, very
few people grasped it or understood it. But when people began to operate on its basis, even though they didn't fully
understand it, they began to change the world. Our whole
modern era was brought about by the discovery of a secret
which was hidden in nature until the time when Einstein
stumbled upon it. There is much yet to be learned, even in
this realm. But how much more are there great riches in store
for us who will give some time and thought and effort to
grasping this great secret which Paul sets before us here—
the ultimate secret behind all things: the mystery of Christ!

In this next sentence he gives us a brief summary of this great mystery:

> . . . the mystery of Christ . . . was not made known to the sons of men in other generations as it has now been revealed to his holy apostles and prophets by the Spirit; that is, how the Gentiles are fellow heirs, members of the same body, and partakers of the promise in Christ Jesus through the gospel (Eph. 3:4-6).

The first thing he says about the mystery is that it has been partially hidden in the past. That is, great men of God in the Old Testament did not fully understand this mystery. As Paul looks back upon the lives of these great men—Moses, David, Isaiah, Jeremiah, and others—he says that though they understood much, though they looked into the future far beyond our own day and God showed them what the end of all things would be, nevertheless they did not completely understand this mystery. The secret was hidden to men of past ages. When did it begin to open up? The answer is, in Jesus Christ. The Lord Jesus himself began to unfold fully the mystery. I refer you to Matthew 13:34-35, where it is recorded that our Lord spoke these amazing words:

> All this Jesus said to the crowds in parables; indeed he said nothing to them without a parable. This was to fulfill what was spoken by the prophet:
>
> > "I will open my mouth in parables,
> > I will utter what has been hidden
> > since the foundation of the world."

Our Lord, then, began to unfold this mystery, to tell us things that were hidden from the very foundation of the world. But God needed to prepare human beings for the unfolding of this secret. He got them ready for it through the rituals and symbols in the Old Testament—the giving of the law and the sacrifices—which helped them, and us, to understand that we human beings have something inherently wrong with us which cannot be cured by our making a few good resolutions. Rather, it is something so drastically and terribly and deeply wrong that the only thing that can cure it is death itself. God had to prepare our race to be able to grasp that fact and to be ready to believe it. But even then he had not fully revealed this mystery. A little was revealed in the past in the shadows and rituals of the law, but the great secret was kept hidden.

But it has now been revealed, Paul says, "to his holy apostles and prophets by the Spirit." There is a line of teaching called "ultra-Dispensationalism," in which certain teachers (who are genuine believers in Christ) teach that only the Apostle Paul knew this secret, that to him was given the privilege of unveiling it for the first time to human minds and hearts. But as we have already seen, it was the Lord Jesus who began to unveil it. And as Paul himself says here, it was made known to all the apostles and prophets, i.e., the writers of the Scriptures such as Luke and James and others who were not apostles, but prophets. In the closing verses of Romans 16 there is a very clear statement on the unveiling of this mystery:

> Now to him who is able to strengthen you according to my gospel and the preaching of Jesus Christ, according to the revelation of the mystery which was kept secret for long ages but is now disclosed and through the prophetic writings [i.e., the Scriptures] is made known to all nations, according to the command of the eternal God, to bring about the obedience of faith—to the only wise God be glory for evermore through Jesus Christ! Amen (Rom. 16:25–27).

Now we come to the actual mystery itself. It consists of this great truth: That the Gentiles are fellow heirs, members of the same body, and joint partakers of the promise in Christ Jesus through the gospel. Here Paul does something that he does frequently (and only the Apostle Paul does this)—he coins words. He runs out of language, is unable to put what he wants to say into the words at his disposal. So he invents new ones by putting words together. Here he makes up three words which you find nowhere else in the Greek New Testament. They are, literally: joint-heirs, joint-bodies, and joint-partakers. When they come to Christ, Jews and Gentiles together are joint heirs, joint members of one body, and joint partakers of the promise. What is he talking about?

Breakthrough

Well, in those three terms we have the answers to our greatest struggles. "Joint-heirs" has to do with possessions. Here he is touching the whole problem of man and his universe, man living in a natural world, the dominion (or lack of it) of man over that world, and the reason why we cannot solve our ecological riddles. The answer, as is detailed in other places in Scripture, is that the old creation which has existed since the beginning of time is gripped by an unbreakable law, which Paul calls "the law of decay" in Romans 8. It is The Second Law of Thermodynamics, if you want the scientific term for it, the *law of entropy*. This law states that energy is becoming less available, everything is running down, deteriorating. We cannot break this law. This is why the ecological problems of today are unsolvable. There is no way we can break through this law.

But Paul says that in Christ the breakthrough has occurred. In Christ, God is beginning a new creation, one that lives by a wholly different principle and is not subject to this law. And this creation has already begun! The thing which was not taught in the Old Testament was the resurrection of Jesus and the effects of it in our lives right now. In the Old Testament there is very little reference to the resurrection of the body. There are a few references—just enough to establish the truth so that the Old Testament believers knew there was life beyond death. But they didn't know what kind of life, what it would be like. This was hidden from them. They died in hope, but that hope was not very well-defined.

The one thing they did not know at all was that the life beyond death, resurrection life, could be made available to us while we are still living. They never understood this, and you will never find that taught in the Old Testament in those terms. But this is what the apostles were teaching—that God has already broken through the old creation and, right in the midst of the old, he is creating a new. Men and women today can live on the basis of this new creation.

We can even learn how to handle our environment on the basis of this new creation. Christians have the answer to the ecological crisis. Dr. Francis Schaeffer has written a book called *Pollution and the Death of Man,* and related this subject to the Christian answer, the only answer to these problems. What we are to inherit from God, ultimately, is the world. Paul tells us, "All things are yours, whether Paul or Apollos or Cephas or the world or life or death or the present or the future, all are yours . . ." (1 Cor. 3:21-22). And the book of Hebrews tells us that we do not yet see all things subject to Christ, but we do see Jesus, the One who has been made heir of all things, and in him we share that heirship, so that one day all things subject to this new law will be ours. One day there will be a reversal of the law of decay, and all things will begin to pick up energy again and be renewed, revitalized, in tremendously increasing degree.

In the realm of relationships this is already true. This is the struggle of humanity which is answered by our becoming "joint-members of one body." Why can't we get along with one another? Why do we fight each other? Why are there so many family breakups? Why is there so much hatred and resentment and bitterness and malice? It is because when we are still living in the old creation those things are inevitable. If you fulfill the flesh, there is no way by which you can keep from living in disharmony with people around you. Ah, but in the realm of the Spirit the breakthrough has already occurred. When we begin to "walk in the Spirit," as we understand what that phrase really means, then we can love, forgive, and begin to reach out to others. The whole experience of life is transformed, right now.

Finally, the Apostle touches on the matter of power: "partakers of the promise." The promise concerned the giving of the Holy Spirit—that God's Spirit himself would live in us and empower us to do everything God want us to do. Any time we know there is something we ought to do, something that would be right for us to do, but which we don't want to do—if we then cast ourselves in helplessness upon the Lord Jesus and trust his word, we can assume the power of the Spirit to do that thing. The power of the Spirit will always come flowing through right at that point, to enable us to do what otherwise we could never do.

This is Paul's explanation of the great mystery. It is a breakthrough, a new and marvelous way of life which has already begun in our experience, and which, ultimately, will solve all the problems facing humanity. The remarkable thing about it is that you can experience it right now. In Colossians 1:27 Paul puts it this way: "Christ in you, the hope of glory." It is the only hope man will ever have of living according to the glory God designed for us when he created man in the beginning.

The present "civilization" we are living in—secular life, with its politics, its education, its legislative system, its reportage of news events—can be likened to a cocoon, clinging lifeless to the branch of history. But inside that cocoon, God is working a metamorphosis. A transformation is taking place. And one of these days that cocoon will open, in the springtime of the world, and a new being will step out—a being which is being created at this time right within the cocoon.

Program for a Caterpillar

This is the great parable that God teaches us in nature. Did you ever wonder why caterpillars crawl on the ground? Why don't they run around on four legs? They are intended to be a picture of life in the flesh, the natural human life. Everything that lies in a caterpillar's path is a horrible obstacle over which it must painfully crawl. It cannot see very far, and doesn't know which turn to take. This is an apt description of the way we live our lives as natural human beings.

But God has a program for a caterpillar. He has "a wonderful plan for its life." I don't know if anyone has told the Four Spiritual Laws to a caterpillar, but the first point would be, "God loves you and has a wonderful plan for your life." What is it? "That you'll die, that you'll come to the end, that

somehow all your old life as a caterpillar will decay and you
will be left lifeless in a cocoon of your own spinning, hanging
on a limb, and apparently it will all be over." But it isn't over.
Right in the midst of that death something happens. We
don't really know what it is. Nobody has ever found out what
goes on inside a cocoon that transforms a caterpiller into a
butterfly. But we know that one of these days, when the sun
begins to shine, all these dead-looking cocoons will begin to
break open, and beautiful creatures will emerge, designed no
longer for life on the lower level, crawling along over every
obstacle, but able to rise above them, able to spread their
wings and fly as an expression of beauty and joy throughout
the world. This is God's lesson regarding what he is doing
now. The cocoon is the old creation, and in the midst of it
the new is taking shape. And the great mystery is that we can
live in that new creation right now.

This may seem like old stuff to you, for unfortunately these
words have come so frequently to our ears that we've lost
the impact of them. But I hope you can go back and think
again of the breathless wonder of this great mystery which
Paul declares to us—how in Jesus Christ we can step out of
the old, even now, into the new creation. The effects of it
can be felt in our relationships with others, in our inner attitudes, in our treatment of the environment, in our enjoyment of the world of nature around us and, ultimately, in
the power of the Holy Spirit imparted to us to make us live
as we ought to live, in the fullness of joy and peace and life
and glory, rejoicing before God. One of these days springtime
will come to the world, and when it comes, what God has already been preparing will then become manifest.

But don't wait until that time to get on the bandwagon; it
has already started. The great mystery is that it has already
begun. You are either a part of the new creation now, or you
are a part of the old; one or the other, but never both. You
may live now as a member of the new creation—in the midst
of the old, but not part of it any more—"no longer strangers,
no longer foreigners," says the Apostle. You have broken with
all that. Therefore live life as members of a new race. Stop

going on in the old way. Don't go on any longer subject to the heartache and misery and malice and hatred and resentment and oppression which comes from the old creation. Rather, break loose and be free in Jesus Christ. When you do, you will understand the practical import of this fantastic mystery which is at the heart of all life, and which God will begin to unfold to us more and more as we go on, until it simply "blows our minds" with the wonder of what is waiting for us.

I don't know how you think of yourself, but I know that it helps me greatly to personalize these great truths, to remember that where God wants the application finally to be made is in our hearts, in our lives, in our families. We are a new creation in Jesus Christ. We are no longer part of the old but part of that new program which is waiting for the dawn of a new world. May God help us to make it personal in our own lives.

16

SECRET RICHES

Ephesians 3:7–12

The glory of God's plan for man has been revealed: In Christ, Jew and Gentile alike are joint-heirs of redeemed nature, joint-members of his body, and we share together in the promised Holy Spirit. Paul continues now to unfold something of the implications of this great mystery:

> Of this gospel I was made a minister according to the gift of God's grace which was given me by the working of his power. To me, though I am the very least of all the saints, this grace was given . . . (Eph. 3:7–8).

There is a sense of wonder as he writes these words. The Apostle mentions two things here, at which he never ceased to be amazed. One was the value of the gift God had given him. This gift, which opened to him his tremendous ministry, came to him, he says, by the grace and power of God.

In 1 Corinthians 12 and Romans 12, Paul describes the gifts of the Spirit, which he says are given to every believer, to everyone who is a member of the new creation in Jesus Christ. This is quite in harmony with what God has done in the old creation. When we were born into this human life, this natural life, we received certain gifts. We call them talents. Perhaps you are musically inclined or artistic. You may have leadership abilities. Maybe it is in public speaking, or writing, that you do well. The various talents are part of God's gifts to Adam, and, in his fallen nature they have been passed on to us. Therefore it is only right that when there is a new creation, a new man, he too should be given talents. Just as you discover and fulfill your natural life by discovering your natural talents, so you fulfill your new life by discovering the gifts of the Spirit which God has given to you.

I think it is very likely that this great Apostle had every one of the gifts of the Spirit, and there are several he unquestionably possessed. Here he is referring to the gift of evangelism. When he says in verse 8: "To me, though I am the very least of all the saints, this grace was given, to preach to the Gentiles," the word translated "to preach" really means "to evangelize" the Gentiles. It was the gift of evangelism that drove Paul out and made him long to preach Christ to people at the far corners of the earth who had never heard of him before. He had this hunger within, which is characteristic of the gift of evangelism.

This gift led to his particular ministry, which was to the Gentiles. A gift is the ability to do something, and the ministry is the area in which it is done. It is the Lord Jesus' prerogative to assign that ministry to every one of us. You have gifts, if you know Jesus Christ. Once you discover your gift, the Lord Jesus will lead you into the place to exercise that gift, which is your ministry. Every believer ought to have a ministry, because the church functions as God intended it to do only as each one of us puts into operation the gifts the Lord Jesus has given us. Both Peter and Paul had gifts of evangelism, but Peter's ministry was to the Jews and Paul's was to the Gentiles. You may have a ministry to children, while others might have a ministry to older people. Some will be led to Blacks, others to Chicanos. But any particular gift can be exercised in all of these ministries, you see; the gift opens the door to the ministry. Paul never got over the wonder of that gift. What a glorious thing it was, he said, that God had given him the great gift to preach this tremendous message to men who had never heard the good news before.

Progress in Humility

The second thing he never got over was the weakness of his own person. Notice his language here: "To me, though I am the very least of all the saints, this grace was given . . ." (Eph. 3:8). I know some people think Paul is merely being polite here, depreciating himself, as we might. But I am sure that the Apostle felt deeply in his heart what he put into words. He is not looking back to when he was a Pharisee. This is a present assessment of his worth; Paul continually thought of himself as "the very least of all the saints."

I have heard people say of Paul, as they have read some of his writings, "This man is an egotist. He talks about his own holiness and faithfulness, his tenderness and compassion. He says, 'Be imitators of me, even as I am of Christ.'" They are amazed at what they think to be the conceit of the Apostle Paul. But if you really want to know what he thought of himself, here it is. In fact you can detect a gradual change of this Apostle's idea of himself over the course of his letters. In the first Corinthian letter, which was written earlier than this, he says, "I am the least of the apostles" (1 Cor. 15:9); that is, last in a list of thirteen. Here he says, "I am the very least of all the saints" (Eph. 3:8). In fact, he invents a word here, putting the comparative and the superlative together: "I am less than the least of all the saints," which is a considerably lower estimation. But when he wrote 1 Timothy much later, he said, "I am the chief of sinners" (1 Tim. 1:15).

Now that is progress! It is right in line with what our Lord said would happen: "Take my yoke upon you," he said, "and learn from me" (Matt. 11:29). What are you to learn from him? "I am gentle and lowly of heart." Here we are face to face with the phenomenon which is frequently seen in the great leaders and saints of the past. The older they grow the more acute is their sense of sin and personal weakness. They see that what they once thought to be natural strengths are really weaknesses. So if this is beginning to happen to you, you are growing as a Christian.

I remember that when I began my Christian life as a young

man I thought I was very close to being perfect. For the
most part I had a pretty good record. There were a few areas
I well knew were not right, but I thought if God straightened
those out everything would be fine. But gradually God has
opened my eyes to see that in those areas where I thought I
was doing well, I was utterly repugnant in God's presence,
utterly displeasing to him. I have had to learn through the
years that my strengths were really my weaknesses. The great
psychologist Carl Jung says this very well:

> In the second half of life [Some of you haven't arrived there
> yet. But you will, if you hang on], the necessity is imposed of
> recognizing no longer the validity of our former ideals, but of
> their contrary, of perceiving the error in what were previously
> our convictions, of sensing the untruth in what was our truth,
> and of weighing the degree of opposition and even of hostility
> in what we once took to be love.

That is an accurate statement of the experience of those
who begin to see themselves. As Paul began to understand
the full revelation of the mystery which is in Jesus Christ, the
clarity of his knowledge made him able to see himself as he
was. And the more he saw himself the more he said, "I am
utterly dependent upon the grace of God. There is no
strength in me." Some of us are beginning to say with Paul,
"For I know that nothing good dwells within me, that is, in
my flesh" (Rom. 7:18). Only that in me which is of God is
worthwhile.

Fruit of the Ministry

The glory of the mystery is right there: Out of weakness
comes strength. And at the very point when this mighty
Apostle could say of himself, "I am less than the least of all
the saints," he could also go on and describe a fantastically
effective ministry. In these next verses it is set forth in beautiful terms:

> To me, though I am the very least of all the saints, this grace
> was given, to preach to the Gentiles the unsearchable riches of

Christ, and to make all men see what is the plan of the mystery hidden for ages in God who created all things; that through the church the manifold wisdom of God might now be made known to the principalities and powers in the heavenly places (Eph. 3:8–10).

He is saying that his ministry was effective in three dimensions. First, those to whom he preached discovered unsearchable riches in Christ. By that he means that the first effect of the ministry of the gospel is the enrichment of life right now. Wherever Paul preached hearts were changed, hurts were healed, families restored, the bad habits of a lifetime were broken, and joy and hope and love and peace began to come into people's lives. Every place he went Paul formed colonies of whole persons, of healed people who were rejoicing in a wonderful sense of liberty and freedom in Christ. Those are the unsearchable riches of Christ, right now—not in heaven some day, but right now!

The same thing is happening today. One of our pastors who was at home recovering from a severe heart attack picked out a handful of letters from the thousands he had received and sent them to the rest of our staff for us to share in his joy. They reflected the blessings people have experienced as they have been helped by his ministry through the years. There was a letter from a husband who had been set free from heroin addiction and had enjoyed a tremendous change in his home. There was a letter from a young man in the service who wrote to give thanks for all he had been taught through the years. He had never realized it was so important until he was out facing life in a cold, cruel, and miserable world. There was a letter from a former leader of Women's Lib who had found the secret of womanhood in Jesus Christ. There were letters from long-time Christians who were overflowing with the glory of thirty years of living with Jesus Christ.

My mail has been very similar. I want to share with you the opening paragraphs of a letter I received one Christmas from a former member of Peninsula Bible Church who moved away to another area.

This Christmas is very special to me. I will never forget this year. This was the year that the Lord revealed himself to me in a most remarkable way. Last year saw me lose a substantial part of my life's savings in a fraudulent business venture. This year the deteriorating trend continued with problems in my health, my job, and within the church I attend. Then came word that my daughter's marriage was breaking up. All coincided to bring me to a new low. I was really hurting. Everything seemed to be going wrong. And I was in a state of total despair.

At this point I cried out, "Where are you, God? Help me!" He answered my prayer gloriously, and I was filled with assurance. My troubles have not disappeared, but I am able to cope with them, and my understanding of God has expanded. I am joyous. It was totally the gift of God. I do give thanks also to friends who knew my plight—although they didn't know how bad it was—and were praying for me, and to the new pastor of our church, who is very effective. There was also the radio ministry of Christian broadcasts which I listen to as I am on the road 95 miles each day traveling to and from work. I thank God that he is showing me how life is meant to be lived. And my desire now is to live it his way, regardless of outward circumstances. *I know that my Redeemer lives.*

There are the unsearchable riches of Christ. How many thousands, even millions living today could add to this story! That is a part of the unsearchable riches in Jesus Christ, as the glory of this tremendous mystery breaks upon human hearts and people begin to discover how life was meant to be lived in the first place. The story can never be fully told until we get to glory. Only then will we ever know anything of the incredible depths of the riches of Jesus Christ.

To Enlighten All Men

Then Paul speaks of the second dimension of the effect of his ministry—the distribution of a universal knowledge. He says it was given to him ". . . to make all men see what is the plan of the mystery hidden for ages in God who created all things . . ." (Eph. 3:9). Isaiah, in the ninth chapter of his prophecy, predicted that the people who walked in darkness

would see a great light, that upon those who dwelt in the
land of deep darkness the light would shine. Then he added:

> For to us a child is born,
>   to us a son is given;
> and the government will be upon his shoulder
>   and his name will be called
> "Wonderful Counselor, Mighty God,
>   Everlasting Father, Prince of Peace" (Isa. 9:6).

He is the light which illuminates the darkness, which is
exactly what Paul says. The word translated "to make (all
men) see" really means "to enlighten" all men—to bring
light to all men about the plan [literally, "stewardship"] of
this mystery. Paul gloried in enlightening men with this tremendous secret, because he knew that the extent of good
government, of international peace, of law and order, of enlightened education, of control of demonic forces, of true
progress in the realm of technology and science, is propor-
tionate to the degree to which this mystery is known, understood, and believed by men.

The mystery was hidden for ages in "God who created all
things." God has ordained life to this end, and it is he who
enables men to reach out, to learn, to grasp, to understand—
according to the degree to which the secret of life is spread
in a society. You have only to look at the recent history of our
nation to see how true this is. When the light of the gospel
begins to grow dim, anarchy, lawlessness, violence, rebellion,
and revolution begin to increase immediately. Superstition,
occultism, and darkness come flooding back in as soon as the
light begins to dim. God teaches us this on the physical level,
as well. If you light a candle in a dark room you have mostly
darkness with a little light. But in a room where there is
ample illumination, the darkness is completely gone. Let that
illumination dim, however, and the darkness increases on
every hand. Paul knew that the enjoyment of human life, of
pleasures and recreation, is entirely dependent upon the degree to which the gospel penetrates a people. Therefore he

gloried in spreading this word in the dark and weary pagan community of that first century.

We need to understand, as this verse tells us, that this mystery was hidden by God until the world was ready for it. All the ages of history before the coming of the Lord Jesus were simply God's way of getting the world ready for the unfolding of this tremendous mystery—the glory of a man, Jesus, who fulfills the wonder of uniting God and man, and makes the believing man a partaker of the divine nature.

Regarding God's preparation of the world for the cross, Dr. Arthur Custance, a very godly Canadian scientist, says in "Process of History" from *The Doorway Papers:*

> The processes of history have special significance because the crucifixion could not be merely an isolated event occurring in some dark age of lawlessness and barbarism, or in some corner of the earth where knowledge of it might filter back into the world only by accident. It was an event which had to be appropriated, witnessed, and recorded, which had to be performed in an orderly, legal way, according to an accepted standard of behavior and judgment to which mankind as a whole would give rational consent. It had to occur at a time when the event itself would be sufficiently public, one might say publicized, that there could never be doubt about its having happened. It had to come to pass when there was a sufficiently sophisticated and dependable means of communicating the news to a large population that was not merely numerous but fluid, so that word of it could be carried far and wide.

He goes on to speak of the need for a legal code, and for a police force with sufficient strength to prevent a lynching, and a universal language, so the message would be culturally universal. And then he says:

> These circumstances may have occurred repeatedly since that time, and perhaps upon occasion in an even more effective way. But it is almost certain that this was the first time that the circumstances had all occurred together. The Roman Empire guaranteed, at least for a short while, a world ideally ordered as a proper setting, both cultural and legal.

In his letter to the Galatians, Paul put it this way: "When the time had fully come, God sent forth his Son, born of woman, born under the law . . . so that we might receive adoption as sons" (Gal. 4:4–5).

Angels Are Watching

The last thing the Apostle says concerning his ministry is that it had the effect of demonstrating a unique wisdom: ". . . that through the church the manifold wisdom of God might now be made known to the principalities and powers in the heavenly places" (Eph. 3:10). This is to go on now, while the church is being formed. It is a revelation in which these "principalities and powers" are learning something by observing the church. What does he mean? Well, this is one of the instances in which Scripture clearly states that we are surrounded by an invisible spiritual kingdom made up of both demons and angels. In Ephesians 6:12 Paul says that we wrestle not against flesh and blood, but against principalities and powers in the heavenly places—wicked spirits from the very headquarters of evil itself. But we also learn from other passages that angels are watching us. It is as if we are on stage in a great theater, with the angels gathered around in rows and rows, watching us, learning from what is happening here in the lives of believers. In 1 Corinthians 11 Paul says to women that their dress and their demeanor toward their husbands ought to be correct "because of the angels." Angels are watching and learning. What are they learning? Let me share with you another quotation from Arthur Custance:

> The key to the existence of such a universe as this lies, I believe, in the fact that God wished to show forth that aspect of his being which the angels have never comprehended, namely his love, without at the same time surrendering that part of his being which they do comprehend, namely his holiness.

So the revelation of the mystery is essentially the revelation of the love of God—in ways that astound the angels as they learn the tremendous secrets of God's love. This is why the Apostle Peter says in his first letter that our salvation is so tremendous that the angels longed to look into these things. He means that God's incredible love is being demonstrated by the church in such a way as to startle and amaze the angels as they see the manifold wisdom of God.

The word translated "manifold" is literally *many-colored*; the angels see the many-colored wisdom of God through the church. This poetic adjective, very rarely used in the New Testament, relates to the colors of life. Have you ever had a blue Monday? Yes, we all have blue days. And red hours of anger and passion. And golden moments of glory. And dark, somber valleys through which we must pass. And lush, green pastures into which we are sometimes led. All of these, the Apostle suggests, are chosen by the love of the Father. God's love is manifest in all of these hues of life. His many-colors of wisdom are aspects of his love. So, when you go through a blue time, it is God's love that you are learning. God's love chose it for you. When you go through a dark and pressured time, somber and discouraging, the love of God is being manifested there. You may not see it, but God knows how to make it clear. And even the joyful times are manifestations of the many-colored wisdom of God.

As the angels watch us, they see us gradually losing our anxiety. We learn to trust God, to turn from our fears, and to renew ourselves with divine strength, to draw upon God's great and mighty promises in the hour of pressure and danger. As they see this, their praise begins to ring out in amazement and wonder at a God—the One they know as the God of justice, the God of infinite holiness—who is also able to find a way to lavish his love upon the very ones who deserve his wrath. This makes the angels praise God. Charles Wesley captured the wonder of God's love in that great hymn that I love to sing:

> 'Tis mystery all! th' Immortal dies!
> Who can explore his strange design?
> In vain the first-born seraph tries

> To sound the depths of love divine!
> 'Tis mercy all! let earth adore;
> Let angel minds inquire no more.

You can never completely solve the mystery of God's amazing love, manifested in the many-colored wisdom which governs the circumstances of our lives. But it is this that edifies the angels, and teaches the demons how great is the God we serve.

Paul reminds us again that it all comes through Christ:

> This was according to the eternal purpose [literally, "the ordering of the ages"] which he has realized [accomplished] in Christ Jesus our Lord . . . (Eph. 3:11).

In Christ, God has ordered the ages so as to produce the unveiling of this great mystery. This means that all of time and all of history is woven together by the hand of God to bring to pass these great events. Paul and the other Apostles proclaimed it. And now it is our fantastic privilege to declare it among men. Furthermore, Paul says that in Christ "we have boldness and confidence of access through our faith in him" (Eph. 3:12). We weak, frail, fumbling, human creatures are free to come boldly, in confidence, before such a God and to pour out our needs before him. When we do, we find him to be a compassionate, tender, loving Father who is concerned to bring to bear all the power of his omnipotence to work out the problems of our lives. Is there any message greater than this? No wonder this Apostle was so excited and amazed that this message should be committed to him, that he should have the privilege of seeing people discover, through this word, the unsearchable riches of Christ, the universal knowledge of the great secret which explains how to unravel human misery and heartache and problems, thus teaching the heavenly beings truths about God they would never know otherwise. No wonder Paul cried out in amazement at the glory of this mystery.

Perhaps you have never found Jesus Christ as your Lord.

It is quite possible, of course, to have attended church regularly, and to have heard these truths over and over, but never to have made them personally yours. But their whole effect is lost until you, personally, are born again—born into this new creation by faith in Jesus Christ. So you may desire, in the quiet and solitude of your own heart, simply to invite Jesus Christ in, and ask him to be your Lord and your Savior, your Redeemer and your King.

Lord Jesus, we thank you for the glory of this mystery which breaks the power of darkness, sets us free from the kingdom of Satan, and brings us into the kingdom of your love, loosens us from chains and habits which bind us and brings us into the liberty of the sons of God. We pray that we may not keep this secret to ourselves, but will gladly tell the story abroad to others, that they too may find the unsearchable riches of Christ. May our hearts praise your name with such joy and thanksgiving that your heart is delighted, our Father, as you read the thoughts of our minds and the expressions of our hearts. May they be pleasing in your sight. We pray in Jesus' name, Amen.

17

PRAYER FOR A FAILING HEART

Ephesians 3:13–21

Most of us engage from time to time in an evaluation of our activities over a certain period. Especially at the turn of a new year we become aware of certain failures which have occurred in the past year, even though we began with the best of intentions. Somehow things have not gone quite as we expected. We haven't been able to do just what we determined to do. At such times we ask ourselves, "How can I do better? How can I motivate myself to do what I know I ought to do?"

Recently I received a note which put this dilemma rather graphically: "What can be done about the problem of self-discipline? For the twenty years of my life before becoming a Christian, I found myself unable to achieve this. And after two plus years as a Christian, it still eludes me, though there seems to be some reason for expecting it on the basis of Galatians 5:23." The verse the writer refers to is about the fruit of the Spirit. It says that not only will there be love and joy and peace, but also gentleness and goodness and self-control—self-discipline. And so this writer is asking, "How can I have this? There is in Christianity the hope of discipline, self-discipline, but how can I lay hold of it?" This is where many of us struggle—the struggle of ought against is. "I *am* this; I *ought* to be that. How can I do it?"

This is the very problem the Apostle is facing in the closing verses of chapter 3 in his letter to the Ephesians. He is concerned about these believers. The setting of this passage is in verse 13, where Paul says, "So I ask you not to lose heart over what I am suffering for you. . . ." The Christians in and about Ephesus were in danger of losing heart. What does it mean, to lose heart? When an athlete is in an endurance contest of some kind, he presses on and on, though his legs begin to turn to rubber and his breath comes heavily and he experiences real physical pain. But he keeps on going, and when he finishes, we say, "What a great heart he has! He has the morale, the stamina, to stay with it." When you lose heart you lose stamina, you lose morale. You come to the place where you say, "What's the use? Why keep going? I can't make it," and you give up. Paul sensed that was about to happen there in Ephesus. They were about to give up, so he says, "I am concerned. Don't lose heart. The situation isn't the way you think it is." And as we have seen, he teaches them some wonderful truth to show them why they ought not to lose heart. But then he closes with this great prayer:

> For this reason I bow my knees before the Father, from whom every family in heaven and on earth is named, that according to the riches of his glory he may grant you to be strengthened with might through his Spirit in the inner man, and that Christ may dwell in your hearts through faith; that you, being rooted and grounded in love, may have power to comprehend with all the saints what is the breadth and length and height and depth, and to know the love of Christ which surpasses knowledge, that you may be filled with all the fulness of God (Eph. 3:14–19).

The Apostle has dealt with the problem of motivation once before, in chapter 1, and he closes that chapter with a prayer also. In verse 15 he says, "For this reason, because I have heard of your faith in the Lord Jesus and your love toward all the saints, I do not cease to give thanks for you, remembering you in my prayers." Then he goes on to pray that the eyes of their hearts may be enlightened, that the truth may grip their emotions and thus enlighten their minds. He prays that they will begin to see truth not merely as intellectual dogma but as living reality, and that thus they will be motivated to begin to move in the direction God wants. The prayer in chapter 3 picks up right at that very point and goes on from there. For the Apostle makes clear that they need not only light and knowledge to begin, but also they need power to continue. They need not only motivation, but they need resolution to keep going, to stay with it, to stick on to the end. That is the difference between this prayer in chapter 3 and the one in chapter 1. That was a prayer for understanding—understanding that grips even the emotions. But this is a prayer for power—power which keeps you going and helps you to recover from losing heart.

Begin with Prayer

In this prayer the Apostle Paul speaks to someone who is about to lose heart, or has lost heart, someone who says he has reached the depths of depression and despair, and who thinks he is unable to come back to the Lord. What do you do for such a person? Maybe you are there yourself. Maybe you are thinking of someone right now who is there, and you don't know where to start. Then pay careful heed as the Apostle takes us step by step up a grand staircase of endeavor here, step laid upon step, rising constantly, leading us on to the fullest possible experience of Christian vitality. We will look at it in the simple divisions that Paul himself provides— first his prayer itself, and then the great paean of praise which comes at the end. The first step:

> For this reason I bow my knees before the Father, from whom every family in heaven and on earth is named . . . (Eph. 3: 14–15).

Note that he begins with prayer. This is important to emphasize. We need to understand more about what prayer really does and how it works. The Apostle clearly understood this, because he was never very far from prayer for those to whom he wrote and for whom he was concerned. He understood that this was an essential ingredient to the solution of their problems. And not only for them but for him as an Apostle. He needed them to pray for him, and he asked for it again and again. The place to begin when somebody's faith is failing, when they are turning cold and lethargic and dead in their spiritual experience, is to pray for them.

Paul prays earnestly for these Ephesians; he says, "I bow my knees before the Father." It wasn't customary for the Jews to bow their knees in prayer. We think of kneeling as the common posture of prayer, although perhaps not as much these days as a few decades ago. But the Jews usually prayed standing with arms outstretched to God. It was only when something was of deep, intense concern that they bowed the knees or prostrated themselves before God. This is the position the Apostle takes here.

Of course, it really isn't important what your position is. I vaguely remember a humorous poem about a group of Christians who were arguing about this. One insisted that the only way to pray was on your knees. Another insisted that it had to be standing with bowed head. A third asserted that the only way to pray was to be seated in a chair looking up to God. One who till then had been silent told of an incident in which he accidentally fell head first into a well. While he was hanging there upside down, he prayed a prayer which he said was the most effective he had ever prayed! So it isn't posture that is important. Nevertheless, the Apostle stresses the earnestness of his prayer: "I bow my knees in earnest concern for you who are about to lose heart" (see Eph. 3:13–14).

Notice particularly the One to whom Paul prays: "before the Father from whom every family [literally, fatherhood] in heaven and on earth is named" (Eph. 3:14–15). It is not family; it is fatherhood. In other words, God is a Father. He is the very epitome of fatherhood, and every fatherhood in heaven and on earth that deserves the name of father draws its characteristics from the fatherhood of God. He is the archetypal father—the Father from whom all fatherhood takes its essence and its character.

Fatherhood here does not mean paternity. Sometimes we read in the newspaper of a paternity suit wherein a woman sues a certain man, claiming that he is the father of her child. It may be true that he has participated in the conception of the child, and is in that sense the father. But that is a far cry from the meaning of *Father* as Paul uses it here. Sometimes *Father* is used of God in the sense that he is the father of all human beings, and in that sense, paternity is involved.

But the usage of *fatherhood* here evokes concepts of concern and provision and loving guidance and faithful training. The fatherhood Paul is speaking of means a special kind of relationship, with shared pleasures, occasional firm handling, and increasing communion. The Apostle wants you to remember that when you are despairing about your spiritual life or about someone else's, when you are feeling cold and lethargic, and you are about to lose heart, that is the time to turn to a Father. God is our Father, and he is the very quintessence of fatherhood.

Paul describes the Father's resources, all of which can be brought to bear on the problem of our paralyzed will, as "the riches of his glory."

God's glory is God's being, God's person. He himself is his own riches of glory. And when God wants to display his glory he shows you himself. He reveals what he is like—an infinitely loving and resourceful Father. You are not going for help to some cold, distant being, sitting up on some remote Mount Olympus, flapping his eyelids in contemptuous indifference to your needs. You are going to a tender, concerned, loving Father, who is deeply involved with you, who wants you to grow, who is concerned about your welfare, and who will not leave you in some state of arrested development. That is what Paul sets before us as the background of this prayer.

Now he begins to trace step by step the course of recovery from spiritual depression; he prays that:

> . . . he may grant you to be strengthened with might through his Spirit in the inner man . . . (Eph. 3:16).

That is the first step: "strengthened with might by his Spirit [literally] into the inner man." This is not a reminder that the Spirit dwells in the inner man, although that is true. Rather, the idea here is that the Spirit might infuse his own strength into your inner man. What is your inner man? We are certainly familiar with the outer man; we take care of the outer man very carefully. We dress it, we clothe it, we feed it, we comb it, we pat it, we primp it, we wash it, we dry it, we smear it with cream. We are always concerned with the outer man—the body and its needs. But we are also aware that there is an inner man. Many commentators say that the inner man is the soul, with its faculties of reason and emotion and will.

But in 2 Corinthians 5, Paul gives us a clue to what he means by "the inner man." There he says that the outer man is perishing, but the inner man is being renewed day by day. That is, for Christians there is something about us which is getting old, decaying, deteriorating. But there is also something about us which is getting better, getting fresher and more vital, increasing, and becoming richer and deeper and stronger every day we live. And that is what he calls "the inner man."

We know that our soul grows old as well as our body. Minds can become enfeebled by age, and emotions can grow unstable and easily affected. Even the will can become enfeebled, so that we don't have the same resolution and drive and determination we once had. So it is clear that the soul is part of our life linked with the outer man which is perishing day by day. We are getting older, growing senile. I had lunch some time ago with a man my age, and at the end of the meal I paid the bill. I gave the waiter the money and he took the bill away and brought the change back. To my astonishment, my friend helped himself to the change and put it in his pocket. Absent-minded! I realized that I was having lunch with a senile old man! I won't tell you about all the times I do things like that.

But, you see, that is not the inner man. The inner man is the spirit, the human spirit, and it is here, not in the soul, that God begins the work of recovery. Not in the realm of our feelings, in other words, but in what psychologists would call the realm of the subconscious, the deep-seated part of our life, the fundamental element of our nature. You know that when you are really discouraged, really broken-hearted, and have given up, your condition is often described as "dis-spirited." That is an accurate term; you have become *dis-spirited*. Your fundamental nature is dissatisfied, discontent. It is not merely a question of temporary boredom. That would be in the realm of the soul. But this is something which touches the spirit, right at the very deepest level of human life, and you find yourself filled with ennui, with despair and indifference that persists for hours and days on end.

Drink of His Spirit

This is where the recovery must begin. And the Apostle tells us here about the capability of the Creator himself, our loving Father, to give us a fresh infusion of strength by his Spirit into our spirit, the inner man. We are strengthened with might by his Spirit into the inner man. Speaking of believers, Paul says, ". . . by one Spirit we were all baptized into one body [We have been made members of the body of Christ] . . . and all were made to drink of one Spirit" (1 Cor. 12:13). That is what our human spirits are for—they are to drink of the Spirit of God, so that the Spirit of God is able to refresh us and revitalize us. Just as taking a drink refreshes your body, so drinking of the Spirit refreshes your spirit, at the deepest level of your life.

Now, that refreshing work of the Spirit does not begin in the realm of feeling. I want this to be clear, because we are so impatient in this process of spiritual recovery to have good feelings return at once. We seek some instant sense of relief. Well, relief will come, but it doesn't start in our feelings. It starts down at the level of the spirit, and may be nothing more than some consciousness of reassurance that things will work out eventually. We sharply feel what occurs in the soul, but we can only deeply sense, somehow, that things are taking place in our spirit.

But realize that this beginning step is not your responsibility; it is God's. Doesn't that help? You don't have to start it. He does. All that is necessary is that you ask him for it. You ask, or someone else asks on your behalf, as Paul asked for the Ephesians. They could have prayed for themselves, if they had known what to pray for, because a prayer is nothing but a cry of helplessness: "God help me." When we ask on that level, God promises to give.

Remember what Jesus himself taught in that great passage on prayer in Luke 11. At the end of the story of the importunate friend (see Luke 11:5–13), he said, "What father among you, if his son asks for a fish, will instead of a fish give him a serpent?" Would any earthly father do that? Would he tantalize, torture his son that way? "Or if he asks for an egg, will give him a scorpion?" What kind of a father would do anything like that? No father would do that, Jesus implies, and neither will God. "If you then, who are evil, know how to give good gifts to your children, how much *more* [Do you feel the force of his argument?] . . . how much *more* will the heavenly Father give the Holy Spirit to those who ask him!" He is not talking about how to be indwelt by the Spirit, but about how to recover from losing heart. The first step, then, is to ask God to grant you that your spirit will receive a new infusion of strength, that you can drink again of the river of the Spirit of life which is in you, and that your spirit will be restored so that you can begin to operate as God intended you to.

This moves us to the second step, which immediately follows. Paul prays that God may grant you to be strengthened with might through his Spirit into the inner man so that "Christ may dwell in your hearts through faith. . . ." Notice the connection—literally, it is not "*and* that" but "*so that.*" You are strengthened by his Spirit *so that* Christ may, literally, "make his home" in your heart. The strengthening of your spirit results in your sensing the personal presence of the Lord Jesus, as your reborn faith takes hold of his promise once again.

The key to that second step is the phrase "through faith." Why have you been languishing, why have you been growing weak and unable to operate? Because your faith is failing. You are not clearly and sharply believing the reality that God reveals. Your faith is dragging. What the infusion of the Spirit does is to awaken faith, so that you can begin to believe again. And the first thing to believe is the most fundamental fact of Christian life—Jesus Christ has come to live in you. Even yet there may not be much feeling involved. It is just a fact that faith again rests upon Jesus' promise given in the upper room in John 14. Judas (not Iscariot) said to him, "Lord, how is it that you will manifest yourself to us, and not to the world?" (John 14:23). And Jesus answered him, "If a man loves me, he will keep my word, and my Father will love him, and we will come to him and make our home *with him*" (John 14:22–23). Faith is awakened now, as you remind yourself that Jesus Christ lives in you. You are a believer. He has taken up his residence in you. He will not leave you. He is at home in your heart, and you belong to him.

Plants and Buildings

That immediately brings us to the third step. Do you see how Paul is leading us, step by step, back to recovery? ". . . that you, being rooted and grounded in love . . ." (Eph. 3:17). Ah, love! Now feeling is beginning to return. Once again you are beginning to sense something, but it is at the third step, not the first, that sensation comes back. Reassured by Jesus' promise to be with you, you now know that you are loved, and that he cares for you, and that he will not change that relationship. Therefore, your self-identity returns.

In other words, as Paul puts it, you are "rooted and grounded in love." There he is mixing metaphors. Plants are rooted; buildings are grounded. But Paul ties them together as beautiful figures of security. A plant that is rooted is solid. Some time ago we had in our yard a tree which you could knock over by pushing. An agronomist came by and told us it had to be tied down so that it couldn't move until the roots took hold. Now you can push it and it will not move. It is rooted and solid and can withstand the storm and stress. And a building needs to be firmly fixed upon a foundation; otherwise it will shake in the wind and storm.

Paul is simply saying here that we need foundations for our experiences. We can't handle life unless we have a solid foundation, unless we are rooted and grounded in love—in the assurance that God loves us, and has accepted us, that we are dear to him, precious to him. When we know this, then we know who we are. Then we have a sense of well-being. Love always gives us that. A lonely, solitary life is so difficult because there is no sense of well-being. What causes people to jump off bridges and blow out their brains? They don't feel loved. No one appreciates them. No one reaches out to them. But the Christian can find his ground of solidarity and security and love in Jesus Christ.

And when that stage is reached, then we are ready for the fourth step: ". . . that you . . . may have power to comprehend with all the saints what is the breadth and length and height and depth . . ." (Eph. 3:17–18).

Now we are climbing back to power and vitality. This sense of identity gives us power to relate to others—"power to comprehend [or realize] with all saints." Now we can begin to relate to somebody else, to reach out to someone else. And when we do, we will begin to lay hold of the breadth and length and depth.

The Price of Privacy

I want to stress that we are not to live in isolation—that is our problem—but to relate to one another, to "realize with all saints," and not to try to work things out all alone. Many Christians attempt to live in solitary confinement. They resist relating, resist sharing. But that is falling into the trap in which the world lives. The world talks a lot about privacy, longs for privacy, struggles to have areas of life that no one sees. It insists upon having private reserves, areas no one enters. But the price of that is loneliness. You can't have privacy without having loneliness. And if loneliness is your trouble, it is because you are insisting upon being private.

But Christian teaching and doctrine undermine this whole philosophy, because it tells us we are not to be private. We are to be open. We are to "widen our hearts," as Paul puts it to the Corinthians. "Reach out to each other," he says. "Bear each other's burdens. Confess your faults, one to another." The Christian is to have no private areas in his life at all. If he insists upon it, he is defying what God has called him to—the sharing of the body of Christ in openness and freedom, for all to see exactly what we are. As we begin to relate to and to share with one another, then we begin to realize the height and depth and length and breadth.

What does he mean? There are many who have made beautiful suggestions about the meaning of these four dimensions. Some see in them the cross, with its height and depth and length and breadth. Some see them as a description of the love of God. But I think they are a reference to some of the things Paul has already talked about in this letter. The "length" is what he calls in chapter 1 "the hope to which you are called"—that hope which began before the foundation of the world, in eternity past, and reaches on through all of recorded time into the unsearchable, limitless reaches of eternity yet to come. That is the length and scope of God's program. We are caught up in God's vast, cosmic endeavor to bring all things together in Christ. That is the hope to which we are called.

The "breadth" is what he refers to as "the riches of his inheritance among the Gentiles"—the fact that Jews and Gentiles and all men alike are gathered up in the church, without difference or division—black, white, rich, poor, slave, freeman, male, female—it doesn't make any difference. All are one, sharing equally in the riches of Jesus Christ, through the cross.

The "height" indicates where we are in Christ—risen to sit together with him in heavenly places, far above all principalities, all powers, all authorities, in this age and in the age to come. It is the place of authority as a Christian, the place of power to be freed from everything that would drag us down, and to live above all that would twist and demolish and destroy in our lives.

And finally, the "depth" is what he has described in chapter 2 as death, the living death out of which God has called us. In that death we were victims instead of victors, following the course of this age, living unwittingly as directed by the prince of the power of the air, following the passions of the flesh, doing what we thought was right and ending up being wrong in everything we attempted. We were "children of wrath," as Paul described us—"by nature children of wrath like the rest of mankind." Out of that living death—the depths of human depravity—God called us into the heights with Christ.

All of this comes to us as we learn to relate to others. The church has been so barren and poverty-stricken, so narrow and insular, because we have loved to attend services and just sit and listen, but not relate to anyone else. It is only in reaching out to others, "realize with all saints," that we can begin to lay hold of all these great provisions in Jesus Christ.

The next step, now, is "to know the love of Christ which surpasses knowledge . . ." (Eph. 3:19). Think of it—to know the unknowable! How do you do that? We all know how you can feel something you can't comprehend. A baby feels his mother's love. He senses how deeply his mother loves him, and there are times when he won't go to anyone else but his own mother because he knows his mother loves him. But what does a baby understand about a mother's love? So the Apostle tells us that as we begin to lay hold of these great truths we begin to see the love of Christ in everything that happens to us—in our circumstances, in the world of nature around, in relationships, in life itself. Here is where feeling floods in at full throttle; we are simply overwhelmed with the sense of love of Jesus Christ. As we sometimes sing, "Heaven above is softer blue, earth around is sweeter green; something lives in every hue, Christless eyes have never seen."

Finally, Paul gives us the last step: ". . . that you may be filled with all the fulness of God" (Eph. 3:19). Now you have reached the top. And when you have, you have realized the purpose of your own creation. This is what God made humanity for. He made us to be vessels wholly filled and flooded with God himself. Now this is not a condition you attain only once or twice in your Christian life. It is a condition to which we are to return again and again. This is what Paul refers to as being filled with the Spirit in which God is in possession and control of our lives, enriching us, blessing us, and strengthening us. Our faith is strong and vital, and we are reaching out, ministering. And, as Paul puts it earlier, we are God's workmanship and we will discover the good works to which we have been foreordained.

Who is going to do this? You? No, God in you.

> Now to him who by the power at work within us is able to do far more abundantly than all that we ask or think, to him be glory in the church and in Christ Jesus to all generations, for ever and ever. Amen (Eph. 3:20–21).

That is the secret. God in you is able to do more abundantly than all you can ask or think. If you insist upon manipulating life and trying to bring your dreams to pass, the best you can hope for is what you can ask or think. But if you put your case in the hands of this mighty God, and follow these steps, obeying him yourself, and praying for others in this same way, you will discover that though he might take you along ways you don't understand, which at first may seem to be tragic in their nature, nevertheless out of them he will bring you to the place where you stand in amazement and awe at what he has brought into your experience and your life— beyond all that you can ask or think. That is the nature of the God with whom we have to do, and that is the power at work in us right now.

Heavenly Father, we know our human failings. We know our weaknesses. We know that we haven't any adequate strength to stand. But Father, we thank you that if we will take these six steps the Apostle has outlined for us—be-

ginning where he began, with prayer—as faith comes into action again it will lay hold of your promises and begin to move out on them, and we can end up exactly where this passage leads us: "filled with all the fulness of God." We pray that this may be our experience. Lord, we don't want to be weak and faltering Christians. We want to be strong men and women of God—able believers, able to glorify your great name and honor you by our lives. Help us to trust you for the ability, for we ask in Jesus' name, Amen.